I0089639

Fisi'inaua 'i Vaha – A Tongan Migrant's Way

A Methodist Minister Applies Tongan Social Concepts in a New Zealand Setting

Siosifa Pole

Philip
Garside
Publishing Ltd.

Copyright © 2020 Siosifa Pole

All rights reserved.

Contact Siosifa at
email: sifapole@xtra.co.nz

The opinions and theology expressed in this book are the
author's own, and do not necessarily reflect those of the
Methodist Church of New Zealand or the publisher.

International Print edition 2020
ISBN 978-1-98-857251-2

The author and publisher gratefully
acknowledge the financial support of the
Methodist Church of New Zealand

Philip Garside Publishing Ltd
PO Box 17160
Wellington 6147
New Zealand

books@pgpl.co.nz — www.pgpl.co.nz
PDF, Kindle & ePub editions also available

The front cover carving
of traditional Tongan double canoes is by:
Naufahu Po'uli Kae 'Eva Namoa Ve'ehala

Contents

Preface

One of the unexpected gifts of the Covid-19 pandemic which sent the whole of New Zealand society into lock-down has been our sudden exposure to silence. The roar of traffic ended abruptly, plunging us into a profound quiet in which for the first time for many years city-dwellers were again able to hear the sound of birdsong. The distinctive calls and chatterings of tui, kereru, kaka, bellbirds and others rang out with something of their original clarity, though it is chastening to remember that early settlers, rowing up Otago Harbour, could not hear each other's voices because of the deafening avian uproar coming from the forest-lined edges of the water.

Now, in the eerie silences of a post-colonial, post-Covid world, we can in this challenging collection of essays hear the voice of a modern Tongan religious leader exploring with us, his readers, what it is to inhabit two island worlds – the village life and culture of Tonga and the urban life and culture of two New Zealand cities, Auckland and Dunedin. Always speaking from a close sense of gathered family connections and gifted with an undiminished delight in the natural world around him, he proudly brings the words and images of his Tongan background into a conversation that has been developing for many years among Christian communities in this much-colonized land.

How shall we speak of our faith, distant as we now are in time and space from the origins of that faith? Ancient creeds and antiquated theological ideas are failing in a modern society that is now multi-faithed, multi-cultural, multi-lingual and – at least among older European settlerdom – predominantly secular. What new resources of language and image, of cultural values, can we discover to replace exhausted words, exhausted ideas? In these essays we can discover the kind of fresh theological insights and expressions of faith we need to rejuvenate our thinking and our language of faith.

The Covid-time imperative, 'be kind to each other', the rapid spread of Maori terms for family and relationships, the remarkable outpouring of compassion and sympathy for Muslim communities attacked by right-wing extremists point to a period of moral and social change which is transforming our whole population at a time when both its coherence and its wellbeing is greatly imperilled by major events thousands of miles away from us. Not to speak of profound climatic changes, as our earth adjusts to a warming which is at least in part due to our own activity.

Into this newly fragile world and to a post-Covid society, picking itself up while beyond its shores most countries are still struggling to contain the pandemic, the Reverend Siosifa Pole brings his own insights, grounded in his own experience of Pacific life. Ocean-derived metaphors of double-hulled canoe rowers, of sand and reefs and the movement of tidal change, as well as his discussion of important topics such as child poverty and victimisation, the suicide rates among young people, the need for periods of relaxation and rest, the importance of collaboration rather than competition, ('Team New Zealand,' in Jacinda Ardern's memorable phrase), the necessity of care for the natural world, the idea of sacred space (*tauhi-va*) in human relationships – these demand our attention. His is a voice to be listened to.

I heartily commend this collection to the attention of all New Zealanders of whatever ethnicity or faith tradition. Siosifa speaks of himself as one navigating his own journey into unknown waters, the *vahanoa* (empty spaces) of the future, and in so doing aligns himself with the many other New Zealanders who have suddenly found themselves launched on a similarly exciting yet dangerous voyage.

Emeritus Professor Colin Gibson

Introduction

Te nā koutou, te nā ta tou kātoa, mālō e lelei, talofa lava, bula vinaka, and warm Pacific greetings to all my readers. Firstly, I would like to acknowledge the presence of the people of the land, the tangata whenua of Aotearoa, the Maori people, whom I would like to offer my sincere gratitude and respect for allowing me to have a place and to speak through this book in their land. Secondly, I would like to acknowledge my ancestors who invented Tongan cultural concepts that subsequent generations have used to explore and interpret life in their various contexts. Thirdly, I pay my tribute to the Methodist Church of New Zealand, Te Haahi Weteriana O Aotearoa, for giving me space, through its stationing process, to interact and dialogue with the local contexts where I practised my ministry, and to apply my Tongan concepts to theological reflection that addresses the social issues that affect our people.

Fisi'inaua 'i vaha refers to spray of sea water from the big waves that crash on the double-hulled canoes (*kalia*), in which my ancestors navigated the deep sea to find new lands of opportunities. Sometimes they accidentally drink the sprays of sea water (*inu e fisi'inaua*) in the course of their voyage. *Inu e fisi'inaua* (drinking the sea sprays) is symbolically used to refer to the hardships that we encounter as Pasifika people in our journey to find opportunities in a new land (*fonua fo'ou*). *Vaha*, refers to the deep ocean. It is a space that separates island from island. Sometimes we call that space *vaha-noa*, meaning an empty or void space. This in-between space is uncertain, which gives us an opportunity and liberty for exploration. This space has been used symbolically as a place for migrants, like me.

The words of the Free Wesleyan Church of Tonga hymn 499 depict the unknown of the *vaha-noa* and its chaotic nature. The hymn states,

> *"Ko si'etau mo'ui, ko e fu'u vahanoa, mafai 'e hai ke faka'uli he potu ta'e'iloa."*

This can be translated as, "Our lives are in *vahanoa*, who has the power to steer us in this unknown space." Being a migrant in Aotearoa means that I am in the *vaha*, sandwiched between two cultures. I am hyphenated, to use S. Tupou-Thomas' concept of in-between space ("Telling Tales," *Faith in a Hyphen*, 2-3). It means, that to survive in this new space, I must find new ways of adapting and evolving. Using Tongan concepts for theological reflection in the context of Aotearoa enables me to adapt and contribute to theological dialogue in the Methodist Church of New Zealand.

This book reflects my journey of ministry in the Methodist Church of New Zealand over the last seventeen years. This journey was like sailing on double-hulled canoes in the vast Pacific Ocean. During this period, I practised my ministry in various contexts, in which I encountered diverse social issues, that my family, members of parishes I served, and communities that I was part of, confronted. My experiences prompted me to write articles for our Parish bulletin when I was in the Dunedin Methodist Parish, and papers that I presented in Conferences as one of the voices taking part in *talanoa* (story telling) in the theological landscape, as well as in the church. Mine is not the only voice, but one of many voices from the *vaha*.

In 2010, Auckland University accepted me for post-graduate studies and a part of the course requirements was a paper on Biblical Hermeneutics. I learned from this course not only the importance of the Biblical texts and their contexts, but also the readers' contexts and their social contexts. Furthermore, I realised that for many years biblical scholarship has been dominated by Eurocentric concepts and perspectives, which are contrary to my context in which I practise my ministry. I'm not saying that these Eurocentric concepts and perspectives are inadequate, but I guess they are no longer apply to many of our contexts. Many of our concepts are contrary to Eurocentric concepts because they are rooted in our local Pacific soils.

The late Rev Dr Sione 'Amanaki Havea alluded to that in his article, "Christianity in the Pacific Context." 'Amanaki writes, "Pacific theology is an effort to put faith and the Gospel in the local soil and context so that they can exist in a local climate." (*South Pacific Theology*, p. 11) His view point is from a theological perspective but, it can also apply to the context of biblical hermeneutics.

Over those years, I participated at Talanoa Conferences, and Oceania Biblical Studies Association Conferences, not only to present papers, but to hear and learn from theologians and Biblical scholars from the Pacific region, their perspectives and viewpoints arising from their cultural and social contexts. It was certainly an eye opening experience because if our theologies and interpretations are not pertinent to the need of our local contexts, or the contexts of our readers and hearers, then our message would not be relevant.

The chapters in this book reflect a lens of reading and interpretation shaped by both Methodist and Tongan traditions in the context of Aotearoa, New Zealand. This lens speaks of my role as a Methodist minister and a migrant Tongan who practices ministry in Aotearoa. I hope this book will address appropriately social issues that affect us locally and globally.

My hope in writing this book is to empower both lay people and ordained ministers in the Methodist Church of New Zealand and beyond, to develop their own concepts, from their cultural and theological contexts, that will assist them in their reading and interpretation of Biblical texts. Neil Darragh in his book, *Doing Theology Ourselves*, claims that we can create our own theology.

He remarks,

> "Many people nowadays think of 'theology' as something beyond them. It seems to be too difficult, or too abstract, or it's better to leave it to the experts. Somehow, somewhere, someone has misled them. Theology is no more difficult than any of the other life-skills that we can and need to acquire. Those who think that it is too difficult have been cheated – or perhaps it is just that no-one has ever shown them how." (Darragh, *Doing Theology Ourselves*, p. 13)

Although Darragh speaks from a theological standpoint, his comments can also be applied to biblical hermeneutics. In addition, our concepts should not only be used to interpret biblical texts, but must bring out messages that speak about justice and injustice in our community, our nation, our region, and the whole world.

I cannot continue without mentioning those who inspired and supported me in undertaking this project. I owe words of thanks to Dunedin Methodist Parish and especially to Rev Ken Russell, the convenor of the *Connections* column in the Parish Bulletin, for his encouragement to be a contributor to the writing of articles to the column. I acknowledge Professor Colin Gibson, who has written the Preface to this book, for his encouragement and support.

I would also like to convey my appreciation to the organisers of Talanoa Oceania Conference and the Oceania Biblical Studies Association for allowing me to participate in some of our Conferences by presenting papers. I would like to pay a special tribute to my colleagues and friends Rev Dr Jione Havea and Rev Dr Nasili Vaka'uta for their encouragement and inspiration to identify and use Pasifika concepts for theological reflection and biblical interpretation. Some of those works are in the chapters of this book.

I owe words of thanks to my parents and the Tongan community for their constant reminder of the importance of our cultural values and concepts.

I would also like to acknowledge the Media and Communication Endowment Fund Committee of the Methodist Church of New Zealand and Rev David Bush for your financial assistance toward the costs of publishing this book. I owe words of thanks to Philip Garside, the publisher, for his expertise and skill in correcting some of my grammatical errors and editing some of my words.

I also would like to acknowledge my wife, Naomi and my two sons, Solomon, Sekonaia, and my two daughters, Kakala and Naomi Jr for their companionship during the last seventeen years of my ministry. *Malo e kataki pea mo e poupou.* Finally, I would like to give thanks and glory to God who called me to go on this journey.

Siosifa Pole

Review of *Doing Theology Ourselves* by Neil Darragh

Everyone can be a theologian.

Neil Darragh is a New Zealand theologian who teaches at Auckland University's School of Theology.

In the world of theology there is a major shift taking place from traditional and common theologies to "contextualised theology," in relation to the time and space of a particular type of people. Neil Darragh in his book entitled *Doing Theology Ourselves* insists that as people of our own time and place we can produce our own theology in relation to our context.

Out of curiosity, the author saw that the theological concepts that he learnt in the past are anachronistic and do not address the real issues that we now face in Aotearoa New Zealand. Therefore, he argues, that in order to make our theology relevant and meaningful we need to challenge some of the embedded theologies. We have to deconstruct our theology in order to reconstruct it again ourselves to meet our own context.

As a Christian, a theologian, a European and a New Zealander, the author is writing from a background that expresses such a context. However, he clearly indicates that although he has a theological opinion on matters important to him, he doesn't rule out the theological points of view of others. He claims that each person should have the freedom to create a theology that is pertinent to his/her context. Providing this freedom would make theology more profound and diverse.

The word "theology" is derived from two words, *theo* meaning "god" and *logy* meaning "reason." It generally refers to a "reasoning God" or an "understanding of God." It is obvious that our individual context shapes our understanding of God. Whether we know it or not, the influence of our family, our church, our community, our politics and our society have shaped both our understanding of God and our practice of ministry. This new understanding is making theology contextual.

Because theology is determined by the people of a community, everyone has the right to do theology. The assumption that only the academics are capable of creating or producing theology is a false claim. Everyone can create theology in relation to their individual context. Usually people have casual conversations on moral issues, about God, and about the Bible without realising that they are engaging in a theological discussion. Ordinary church goers are doing that at church, during morning tea, lunch time, in the car-park and even in workplaces. Expressing their individual point of view evokes lively theological discussion on a particular issue. In this type of environment everyone is valued and worth listening to. The author argues that our individual theological point of view will influence our faith and our ethics.

In the first chapter, the author suggests that it is possible for everyone to do theology. It certainly needs time and effort to create theology, but the opportunity is available to everyone. Those existing theologies were stepping stones. Our forebears in the faith created theologies that our practice of ministry has built upon. The author calls these existing theologies "implicit theologies." Although these theologies have contributed to the life of the Christian community, they need to be challenged and re-interpreted to make them relevant for today. In doing so, theology will become contextualised to meet the demands of the community. When theology is out of context it is not only out-of-date but has no influence on the community. Theology has to address the real needs of the community.

In chapters two and three, the author deals with the importance of those who are doing theology on general issues that are reflected in their own theology. These issues relate to two worlds. These are:

1. The worlds of our own personal belief that affect our personal understanding of God, and
2. The world where we live that affects our practice of ministry.

On the one hand, the author claims that we inherited words such as revelation, Spirit, creation, life, and community, that affect our understanding of God. On the other hand, are the issues that we face in our world such as health, housing, education, poverty, and employment, which set the agenda for our practice of ministry. The author insists that we cannot have one without the other. However, he argues that to develop a genuine theological approach we have to begin from our contemporary world. He calls that approach, "Our involvement."

In order to create a profound theological concept we need to begin with our real life experience. We have to look for a real issue that affects our community, apply some biblical insight, and then look for a proper action that can restore life.

Writing from a Christian perspective, the author in chapter four carefully discusses the proper use of scripture as a tool for creating contextual theology. He is conscious of the ever present possibility of misusing scripture. This misuse will damage the practice of theology. He suggests that to have a thorough understanding of the scriptures we must look to the world behind the texts or the context of the scripture, before we apply it to our own contemporary contexts. Because the world behind the text is different from ours, we need to interpret the text carefully to address the issues of our contemporary world.

It is obvious that the author is writing from a point of view that is not strange to many contemporary theologians. Because the community determines theology, it is changeable. This opinion offers a powerful message to the Christian community that everyone can be a theologian. The author is pointing us to the importance of the Bible for theological reflection as well as the importance of the community we engage with and practise our ministries in.

There are sources in our local contexts that can assist us to shape a theology that is pertinent and relevant to our community and its needs. We also need to be aware that because everyone has the right to do theology, we have to be open-minded about the diverse theological opinions that we have among us. Our individual contexts will shape our understanding of God and will determine the way in which we practice Christian ministry here in Aotearoa New Zealand.

Tahi Ua: The Changing of the Tides

The church must take the time to respond effectively to the changing tides of politics, values, etc.

It is always refreshing to walk down St Clair beach on a sunny afternoon. On my day off, I love walking on the beach and there I am always aware of the changing of the tides. At the low tide, I can walk on the beach below the seawall at the Esplanade, all the way to St Kilda beach. At high tide, I can't walk where I can at low tide. The sea is high, and the waves roll strongly and crash powerfully into the seawall.

This living experience of the changing of the tides reminds me of the importance of time for the local people in Tonga when they go to the seaside looking for seafood for their sustenance. Usually, the local people of the island go to the sea at the low tide to find seafood. They do it with extra care for their safety and for the sake of their families. While they are looking for seafood in the coral reef, they are aware that the high tide will return. They hurry to ensure that they will have everything that they want. When the high tide rises, they return home with their catch and watch for the next low tide. If the low tide happens twice in a day the people of the village see this as a double blessing. It means they can go to the sea for a second time and look for more seafood. Two low tides on one day is what we call *Tahi ua*, which means, *two seas*. Those two seas provide more than enough for local people for their livelihood. This usually happens in the morning and late afternoon. Because of the importance of *Tahi ua* to the survival of our people, I see it as a concept that identifies the inevitable changing of time, the risks, and the opportunities that come with it.

Our life and our movements are controlled by the passage of time. There is a saying, 'Time waits for no person.' In the western world, we use a wrist watch to measure time. It ticks every second, every minute, and every hour. Whatever we do, we are controlled by the ticking of the watch. It means we sleep on time, wake up on time, and start work on time. Our behaviour and actions change according to the changing of time so that there is no confusion or contradiction, nor missed opportunities. In other cultures, they don't rely for their timing on watches but rather in the natural world and human interaction. Just like the concept of *Tahi ua*, movement and action are influenced by the context of where they live and by their interaction with the human and natural worlds.

I had that experience when my lecturer, who is an American, and I had a trip to Tonga in 1995. We came to the capital of Tonga, Nuku'alofa. On our return to my village, we decided to go by bus. We walked onto a bus that would take us, but after 15 minutes sitting in the bus, we were still the only passengers. My lecturer started to worry and asked me the time the bus would leave. I told him that in this place there is no exact time for the bus to leave. The bus can only leave when it is full of passengers, and so we sat in the bus for about an hour before it departed. It was really a learning experience for this American. Time in this context did not depend on watches but on human interactions and relationships. The bus driver didn't leave until everyone from this village was on the bus to return home safely.

In his book entitled, *The Gift of Time*, William McConnell insists that our understanding of time is shaped by our various contexts, despite the clock ticking. He states,

> "We have all noticed that sometimes time flies, sometimes it drags, and other times it just lies there heavy on our hands. That is, our inner time responds differently to the steady pace of the clock, depending on what is happening within and around us." (p. 17)

Whatever our understanding of time, the *Tahi ua* notion reminds us that our actions must change when the tides change. No one has the power to confront or to ignore this change. Our survival will depend on our evolving and adapting to the changing of the tides.

We are in a time when the tides are changing in terms of politics, morality and values, social problems, theology, human conditions, and the natural world. Such tides of change are inevitable, but the church must look for ways to respond effectively and smartly so that it still relevant during these changes. Jesus talks in the gospel about the signs of times and need for us to act wisely. He says,

> "From the fig tree learn its lesson: as soon as its branch becomes tender and puts forth its leaves, you know that summer is near." (Matthew 24:32)

As we approach the General Election, the concept of *Tahi ua* reminds us that we need to take action before is too late, to take risks in order to find successful outcomes, and to also look for opportunities for the survival of our community, our whanau, and our *kāinga*. This means that while we have the time and the opportunity, we must take it with two hands. Don't let this opportunity slip away for it will cost us a lot.

Tangilaulau: Lament for the Loss of Young Lives

*We have too many young lives devastated by domestic
violence and lost to suicide, and we need to break the
silence and cry out in concern.*

I was very honoured and privileged to be one of the presenters at
the Oceania Biblical Studies Association Conference that was held at
St John's and Trinity Theological Colleges. This Conference was held
for two days, on 21 and 22 April. Those two days were enriched by
presenters who offered papers on climate change, land occupation,
war and peace, violence against women, just to name a few.

I had a chance to present my paper on violence against young people
and youth suicide in relation to the lament of Rachel in Matthew 2:16-
18. These issues were not new to the audience and yet these issues
are rarely discussed openly in families and churches. We have too
many young lives devastated by domestic violence and lost to suicide,
which is a serious concern. The community seems silent about these
issues, but we need to interrupt that silence. That was the purpose of
my presentation. In order to interrupt the silence, I suggested that we
need to lament loudly and consistently.

The Tongan word for 'lament' is *tangilaulau.* It can be translated as
'weeping or wailing or crying with murmuring.' It is a type of weeping
and crying which physically and verbally expresses pain by raising
the voice so loud that everyone can hear the heartache and hurt of
losing a loved one. That voice will not be heard unless people attend
to these issues and at the same time intervene to console and to
comfort. Moreover, there will be no consolation if there is no honest
and open conversation and consultation about the loss of life. In that
way, *tangilaulau* is seen as an avenue to express one's honest feeling
toward his/her loss. Furthermore, *tangilaulau* enables a person to
break the silence of pain and hurt.

The concept of *tangilaulau* is the only voice heard in the slaughter of
the children of Bethlehem in Matthew 2:16-18. This passage is part

of the Infancy Narrative according to the author of Matthew's gospel. We are told that Joseph and Mary were warned in a dream by an angel of the Lord to flee to Egypt in order to save the life of their baby Jesus. While they were on their way to Egypt, King Herod sent his soldiers to kill all baby boys under two years old in Bethlehem.

The angel of the Lord didn't warn the mothers of Bethlehem to rescue their children. In addition, no one dared to mourn or to acknowledge the loss of these young lives. There is a complete silence in the text, and also the historical documents from the time about this massacre. Even God seems to remain silent in the text. Warren Carter, a Biblical scholar insists that although God was not involved in Herod's decision; God seems to be powerless to defend these young lives. He remarks, "God predicted it in scripture and permitted it in the present." (*Matthew and the Margins*, p. 86) But there was a voice, from the past (Jeremiah 31:15) and she was a woman. Her name is Rachel. Matthew writes,

> "A voice was heard in Ramah,
> wailing and loud lamentation,
> Rachel weeping for her children;
> she refused to be consoled, because they are no more."

It is a voice from the past that interrupted the silence about the horror of this massacre and the loss of these young lives. The future of this community is gone for they are no more.

Rev Greg Hughson in his unpublished paper, entitled, "A Practical Theology of Suicide (Whakamomori) Prevention," shows annual reports of statistics and graphs of those who died of suicide. In 2007 to 2008 there were 540 deaths from suicide, 2009 to 2010 were 558, 2011 to 2012 were 547, 2013 to 2014 were 529, and 2014 to 2015 there were 569 suicides. The trend of suicide deaths has varied every year but has been increasing dramatically.

The deaths of these young people happened across many cultures and ethnic groups. I was privileged to take part in the remembrance of these lives when I was invited to do a karakia at the Life Matters Suicide Prevention workshop that was held at the Dunedin Town Hall in 2016. I was privileged to be one of the voices to mourn and to acknowledge the loss of these young people who died by suicide and from violence.

It is not only suicide that costs these young lives but also domestic violence. Statistics from the New Zealand Family Violence Clearing-house[1] show the appalling trend of deaths among young people under the age of 20 because of domestic violence. In 2007 there were 14 deaths, in 2008 15 deaths, in 2009 29 deaths, in 2010 13 deaths, in 2011 20 deaths, in 2012 13 deaths, in 2013 10 deaths, in 2014 10 deaths, and in 2015 17 deaths due to domestic violence. Although, some cases are not reported to the Police, these statistics show the horror of domestic violence against young people in our country. It reflects that New Zealand, which has a population of 4.47 million, has one of the highest rates of child abuse among developed countries. Who has the compassion and courage to interrupt the silence?

Janet Frame in her novel entitled *Owls Do Cry*, raised the alarming injustices done to those who were locked in mental institutions in the 1950s in New Zealand. The author shared her own experience of being a patient in a mental institution and the horror she faced as a person by the name of Daphne. She was a victim of abuse and abandonment but was able to break out as a survivor. Janet's story in this novel shows how to resist violence and to fight for justice through compassion and courage. She became the voice for the silent voices in this hostile community.

Tangilaulau provides a way for the voiceless to make their voices heard and known. It is also an avenue for those who grieve, to release their pain and grief, as in the case in Manchester at the moment, of those mourning the deaths of loved ones as the result of the insane actions of a suicide bomber. Rachel's lament *Tangilaulau* in Matthew 2:16-18, became the voice for the mothers of Bethlehem and their murdered children. As members of the Dunedin Methodist Parish, we can be the voice for all those who are victims of suicide and domestic violence. Let's break the silence together.

---

1. https://nzfvc.org.nz/

Taukakapa: A Mount Everest Experience

*The writer compares the life of a Christian with climbing
Mt Everest and the Tongan Taukakapa concept, to aim
high in our personal endeavours.*

Our family was fortunate to have a time out from our busy life in the
Parish ministry last year. I have to thank the members of the Parish
for giving us that space to relax and to reflect on the importance of
family. We always try to find somewhere in the country that can give
us that space. We found it this time in the Waitaki Valley.

We enjoyed our time in two places – the townships of Otematata and
Omarama. The first four days we spent at Otematata and we spent
the rest of our holiday at Omarama. Those eight days were filled
with exploration, discovery, excitement, endurance and learning. To
explore the natural surroundings of the Waitaki Valley we planned
to travel each day a long distance on both tarseal and gravel roads to
various destinations. We travelled up the hills and down the valleys.
At one point we lost our way and ended up in an unknown place
in the country, which reminded us about the nature of exploration.
However, we endured and at the end we found our destination, a
popular sight-seeing place, known in the Waitaki Valley as the Clay
Cliffs.

Clay Cliffs are about 10 km west of Omarama. The Clay Cliffs are
huge pinnacles and ridges with deep, narrow ravines separating
them. The Clay Cliffs are made of layers of gravel and silt, deposited
by rivers flowing from glaciers existing 1-2 million years ago. When
we arrived there, it was windy and raining. This meant that the
way to the Clay Cliffs would be slippery – for it was muddy – but
it didn't deter us! Everyone was determined to walk up to the Clay
Cliffs. When we arrived, Naomi decided to climb up one of the lower
pinnacles. The girls decided to climb too. I was left standing at the
bottom worrying about whether they would safely reach the top,
which they did. As I was watching their determination to reach the
top of this pinnacle, I asked myself whether I would climb? In the end

I decided to climb too. When we descended it was dangerous in the same way as when we climbed up. We arrived safely at the foot of this pinnacle and on our way home, Kakala said to me, "This is our Mount Everest Experience dad." I asked her, "Why do you think that this is our Mount Everest experience?" She answered, "Because it was so difficult and dangerous." I responded to her, "You are right Kakala but it was exciting when we reached to the top." Kakala replied, "That's right Dad!"

This conversation perhaps reflects the kind of experiences that mountaineers and explorers have when they climb Mount Everest, the tallest mountain in the world. No one ever reached the summit of Mount Everest until Edmund Hillary and Tenzing Norgay did on the 29th of May 1953. They experienced a mixture of fear, exhaustion, and frustration but also of joy, excitement, and triumph.

Striving to the summit of Mount Everest exemplifies the experiences of those who are aiming high in their personal endeavours. Aiming high is not an easy adventure. It is a combination of endurance, courage, vision and determination. It involves frustration, uncertainty and risk, but also joy, fulfilment and increased self-belief for those who reach to the top of the pinnacle. As, former United States Secretary of State, Madeleine Albright writes,

> "As you go along your road in life, you will, if you aim high enough, also meet resistance.... But no matter how tough the opposition may seem, have courage still and persevere.[2]

Aiming high reflects the Tongan notion of *taukakapa*, which means stretch and touch. It is a word that derives from picking fruit from fruit trees like coconut, mango, orange, kuava, tava, and many other tropical fruit trees that grow in Tonga. It is a difficult task for climbers to pick the mature and ripe fruit from a fruit tree. In some instances, climbers have to climb to the highest point of a fruit tree or stretch out to the end of a branch to pick a ripe mango or an orange. When the climber is stretching out to pick the fruit it is possible that he or she could fall down. It is not a nice feeling when you fall from a mango, coconut, or orange tree. I had that experience myself a few times! But that is the risk that anyone who wants the best fruit

---

2. https://quoterati.com/authors/madeleine-albright

from the trees has to take. *Taukakapa* envisions determination and courage to strive for the best in the midst of challenges and obstacles. It insists on taking risks in order to achieve a better future and to make a positive contribution.

The notion of *taukakapa* encourages perseverance, determination, self-belief and hope. When someone does their best to achieve that vision, it can be the pinnacle of his/her journey – and that's inspiring.

We are at the beginning of Lent, a Christian Season that began on Ash Wednesday and will conclude at sun-down on Holy Saturday. During Lent, as Christians, we remember the sacrificial life and ministry of Jesus as he began his journey from Galilee and ended up on a cross on Golgotha (the Place of the Skull). It was not an easy journey. He was tormented and mocked, but he endured to the end. But Jesus' story didn't end on the cross.

Three days later his tomb was found empty. Christ was risen from the dead. During Lent, we are reminded of our own discipleship as we attempt to follow the footsteps of Christ. These footsteps of Christ in our lives ideally will bear the marks of justice, love, compassion, peace and hope. We are called to follow Christ not only to the highest point, but also to the lowest point. The lowest point is the edge or the margin, where the most vulnerable people of our society live: the poor, the neglected, the homeless and the widower. The *Taukakapa* concept encourages us not only to aim high in our personal endeavours, but also drives us to reach to the edge and the margin of our society with the love of Christ and touch them with compassion. If we can do this during Lent, this will be our Mount Everest experience.

Vahanoa: A Space for Opportunities

*The ocean is a metaphor for the unknown future and the
risks and opportunities it brings.*

Vahanoa is made out of two words, *vaha*, meaning space, and *noa*,
meaning empty or zero. The notion of *noa* in this context is not about
a void but about the unknown. When these two words *vaha* and
noa are joined together, they become *vahanoa*, meaning unknown
or uncertain space. When we speak of *vahanoa* we refer to the deep
ocean, a space of the unknown and uncertainty – but at the same
time a space that can provide new opportunities.

On Monday, I went to St Clair beach for a walk as I usually do on
my day off. It was a fine day, but it was very windy, which causes
a rough sea. The big waves rolled in and crashed on the seawall of
the Esplanade causing excitement for the passers-by. I decided to sit
down on one of the seats. I looked to the deep ocean with fear and
wonder. I felt fear because of the big waves and strong winds, which
can damage boats and cost lives.

I was immediately reminded about the Lampedusa Cross (a wooden
cross made from pieces of a boat that was wrecked off the coast of
Lampedusa, Italy in 2013) and what it represents – the danger of
crossing the deep ocean. There are unknown obstacles that voyagers
unexpectedly face as they navigate their way in the deep ocean. It
prompts everyone to prepare for those moments. But I was also
looking with awe at the vast space that the deep ocean provides for
voyagers and explorers who are searching for new opportunities
at the far end of the world. That reminded me of the courage and
determination that my ancestors had as they travelled from Southeast
Asia on rough seas, searching for lands of opportunities.

Vahanoa can also refer to unknown land space and unknown territories
that people migrate to and settle. Because they have moved from the
familiar and the known, to the unfamiliar and the unknown, they
are regarded as people who are settled on the *vahanoa*, an unfamiliar

space. Obviously, every migrant who settles in a new land will face the reality of the unknown and unfamiliar challenges. These challenges can pose a threat to any migrant's integrity and cultural identity. Yet, settling in a new land can offer new opportunities to pursue for the betterment of our lives. I believe that to be the experience of most of the refugees who settled in our city recently. The new destination where they have now settled, offers them hope and a better future for their children.

Although *vahanoa* can pose a threat to those who travel across it, we cannot deny the opportunities that it provides for those who have courage and the vision of a better future. It is that kind of hope which gives travellers the mindset to stay positive during hardship.

We are all travellers in one way or the other and we are always in the middle of a *vahanoa* experience. Sometimes, we give up hope and optimism, rather than trekking on, with courage and an expectation of new opportunities. John O'Donohue in his book, *To Bless the Space Between Us*, writes,

> "Consequently, when we stand before crucial thresholds in our lives, we have no rituals to protect, encourage, and guide us as we cross over into the unknown. For such crossings we need to find new words."

But I believe finding new words is not good enough without also finding new actions and new meanings.

I am always impressed with the story of the calling of the first disciple – as the author of Luke's gospel wrote in Luke 5:1-11. Jesus said to Simon, "Put out into the deep water and let down your nets for a catch." Simon answered, "Master, we have worked all night long but have caught nothing. Yet if you say so, I will let down the nets." The result of letting down their nets in the middle of uncertainty and the unknown was that they caught so many fish their nets were almost destroyed.

This story is an example of those who are in the *vahanoa* experience. They are frustrated and stressed, for there is no positive outcome from their hard work for the whole night. It is understandable that they were inclined to give up hope altogether. Yet, the words of Jesus stirred them to maintain their hope and helped them to realise that there were still opportunities, yet to be discovered, in the midst of their chaos. Furthermore, it was his failure that gave Simon another opportunity to embrace a new action and to find new a meaning for his life and his career.

It feels to me that our Parish is, in some ways, going through a *vahanoa* experience since the closing celebration of our Wesley Methodist Church last Sunday. Like Simon Peter, we are all frustrated and stressed because we have worked so hard, with apparently little result. To add to our frustration, our membership is declining, and our congregations are ageing. We are obviously at a crossroad. Can we still have hope in the midst of our uncertainty? Can we still find opportunities for growth, in the midst of our frustration?

Our Methodist Church President, Rev Prince Devanandan, reminded us last Sunday that we must look beyond the four walls of our church buildings for opportunities for mission. His words reiterate the well-known saying of John Wesley, "The world is my parish." *Vahanoa* reminds us of the challenges which we face in our journey into the unknown, but it also reminds us of the hope we are still yet to discover in our explorations. The Advent Season reminds us that we must be hopeful in our waiting for the coming of Christ to be with us, as our Emmanuel (God is with us). We are not alone.

So, every time you go to St Clair beach, I hope you will enjoy looking toward the deep ocean – *vahanoa*. Deep oceans provide vast opportunities and challenges for explorers and navigators. Let's ask God, and each other, where best to cast our nets in the midst of all our uncertainties.

Whose Footprints Shall We Follow?

*If we follow Jesus, he will make us his followers to live out
his compassion, his peace, his love, his justice and his care.*

Last Monday I went for a walk at St Clair beach and as soon as I put my
feet on the sand, I saw many footprints of different sizes and shapes
and they faced in different directions. It immediately prompted me to
think of two things, firstly the importance of footprints and secondly,
following.

In looking at many footprints, I asked myself a familiar question,
"Whose footprints should I follow?" I guess that although footprints
and following are two different aspects, yet they are inseparable. They
are inseparable because following happens when there are footprints.
Without footprints it is hard to follow or to find direction. But at the
same time, it is hard to follow when there are so many footprints and
especially when they are scattered in different directions. We have so
many footprints in the church, in our society, and in the world that
we are sometimes confused about which footprints to follow.

We have heard many different voices in church argue about different
theologies and styles of worship that we should adopt as a way
forward to build a church that might be vibrant and meaningful.
We have heard in politics, different voices claiming that their party's
policies will work for the benefit of all people in Aotearoa. We have
heard different voices from leaders of the powerful nations in the
world about their strategies to combat terrorism and to create peace.
It is interesting to hear their rhetoric, which is not always the same
as their actions. Different people have taken a lead in their different
pursuits and have left their footprints, expecting people to follow.

I was privileged to be present at two events on Wednesday 24 August,
which both focussed on the value of peace. The first one that I
attended was the annual Dunedin Abrahamic Interfaith Group and
Otago Tertiary Chaplaincy Peace Lecture, which was presented by
Imam Afroz Ali. The topic of his presentation was, *Between Law and*

Spirituality: Islam's legal basis for its spirit of peaceful coexistence.[3] He spoke passionately about the value of peace, which was something that we all need to share equally in our diversity. Imam Afroz Ali stressed frequently in his presentation the point that we have a responsibility for building a world for our future generations to live in and enjoy. In other words, we need to leave behind footprints that generations to come can follow which will help them to be able to find life.

On the same evening, I rushed to the Mornington church to hear Colin Gibson's presentation on Karl Jenkins, a composer and a conductor. I was impressed with Jenkins' music especially his emphasis on peace and his insistence against war. Colin summed up his presentation by showing a DVD of Jenkins' performance on stage with his orchestra of *The Armed Man: A Mass for Peace.* While the orchestra performed there were slides showing in the background of horrible pictures of people suffering during World War I and World War II. As I was enjoying Jenkins' music at the same time watching the devastation effect of war, I asked to myself these questions, "Haven't we learned a lesson from the footprints of tyrants and dictators? Will we learn the horror of war before it is too late?

We have a duty to future generations and the kind of footprints we leave behind is surely the legacy which will determine their future. Some of you might have seen or heard about the poem *Footprints in the Sand* and its emphasis. The poem was about a person who had a dream that he was walking along the beach with the Lord. While they were walking, this person noticed that sometimes there were two sets of footprints, other times there was one only. He complained to the Lord saying,

> "You promised me Lord, that if I followed you, you would walk with me always. But I have noticed that during the most trying periods of my life there has only been one set of footprints in the sand. Why, when I needed you most, have you not been there for me?"

---

3. http://www.dunedininterfaith.net.nz/peaceLecture16.php

The Lord replied,

> "The years when you have seen only one set of footprints,
> my child, is when I carried you."

The image of footprints in this poem reflects care, love, and compassion. It's really portraying an image of a mother's womb where a child is carried, nurtured, and cared for months before he/she is born. It articulates the nurture of compassion that Imam Afroz Ali referred to in his presentation. The way he defined the word *compassion* from an Islamic perspective is equivalent to the love and protection provided by a mother's womb. He claimed that to be compassionate we have to look to our own mothers. This claim is true in my own experience as I reflect on my mother's compassion toward us children. Without my mother's compassion I wouldn't be here today. She left with me footprints of compassion, love, and care that I should follow and leave behind for the generations to come.

Last Sunday we celebrated Youth Sunday. In the two services that I took with the Mosgiel Lay Team in both Mosgiel and Wesley churches, we emphasised the importance of children and young people in our church. They are the present and future of the family, the nation, and the church. If there are no children and young people there will be no family, no nation, and no church. But if there are children and young people, we need to be sure about the kind of footprints we leave behind for them to follow.

Jesus invites those who answered his call to discipleship to follow him. In the gospel of Matthew 4:18-22, Jesus called four of his disciples and he said to them, "Follow me and I will make you fish for people." We see in this calling statement the vitality and relevance of *following* and *making*. If we follow Jesus, he will make us his followers to live out his compassion, his peace, his love, his justice and his care.

This is the longing of the composer of hymn 514 in *With One Voice* and in the last verse he writes,

> "Lord, let me see your footmarks
> and in them plant my own;
> that I may follow boldly,
> and in your strength alone;
> O guide me, call me, draw me,
> uphold me to the end;
> and then in heaven receive me,
> my Saviour and my friend."

Do we know whose footprints we follow?

Whenever you have a chance to go for a walk at St Clair beach, reflect carefully on whose footprints you will choose to follow, not only on the beach, but in your life journey.

Inu e Fisi'inaua: Drink from the Waves' Spray

A Concept of Endurance in Times of Great Challenge.

*Tongan concepts of resilience and mission are derived
from seafaring in the South Pacific. Church leaders
also need to be resilient, create a vision for growth and
maintain our mission which is to reach out
with the love of Christ.*

It feels fresh to take a walk at sunset around St Clair beach when the weather is fine. My body and mind relax, and both enjoy the cool breeze of the easterly wind. I immediately feel at peace and renewed, as I meditate on the wonder of God's creation.

It is a different experience if you walk around the beach on a wild and windy day. The waves are getting bigger and they roll down and splash on the seawall of the Esplanade and spray over the top of the wall. Those who walk on the top of the seawall like myself are confronted by the spray from big waves. The spray from the waves goes up high above the seawall. Sometimes those who walk on the top of the seawall accidentally sniff or drink the sea water that comes up from the big waves. This short experience at the St Clair seawall reminds me of this Tongan saying, *Inu e fisi'inaua* (drink from waves' spray/sea-water).

"Drinking from the spray of waves," is the experience of sailors and navigators as they sail their boats in the sea on long distance voyages. Our ancestors were known for their experience in the South Pacific Ocean. They didn't have the technology and tools that European navigators and explorers had, but they had their experience and knowledge about the circle of nature as their direction. They relied on their experience of the sun, the wind, the stars, the moon, and ocean currents.

In his book *We, the Navigators*, David Lewis remarks on the experience of the Polynesian people of sea voyaging. He states,

"One essential part of this complex, often at the core of it, is an image of the outrigger canoe and the heroic men who comprise its crew, sailing intrepidly over uncharted seas to yet undiscovered isles."

They travelled between islands on their big wooden outrigger or doubled-hulled canoes looking for food and exploring new lands. As they travelled by sea on the route to their destination they were usually confronted by strong wind and big waves. Those experienced navigators and sailors endured these challenges by standing firm in their positions while their boat was tossing around. They were smashed and tossed by the waves and sometimes they drank the sea water as they faced those challenges. Despite those challenges, they would never give up, because the survival of the passengers depended on their expertise and endurance.

Those experienced navigators and sailors are known as *kaivai* (water-eaters) because they usually consume the sea water from waves' spray as they carefully navigate their boat to arrive safely at their destination. They don't mind the salty taste of the sea water because their main goal is to reach their destination and accomplish their mission.

Inu e fisi'inaua is a Tongan concept, which originates from the experience of the seafarers and navigators as an encouragement for those who face great times of challenge, not to give up. There are three important factors which would encourage a navigator to endure such a rigorous voyage. Firstly, the survival of the passengers, secondly, to accomplish the mission, and thirdly, to enable the mission to continue on.

A navigator's most important priority is to save the lives of his passengers and he would take all the steps necessary, while at sea, to safeguard his passengers. He would always draw on the best of his ability to fulfil the mission that he is aiming to accomplish. He would also see that arriving at his destination is not the end of the mission but is part of a long journey to accomplish more in the future. These three factors would empower a navigator or sailor to endure the rough sea and to drink the salty water from the waves' spray (*inu e fisi'inaua*) of the ocean. He would not and will not give up until he achieved all these factors.

The concept of *inu e fisi'inaua* is at the heart of the gospel and Christian theology. Discipleship is an integral part of the gospel. The concept of *inu e fisi'inaua* can help us to draw meaning out from the gospel that shapes our theology. In the gospel of John 3:16, we have these words,

> "For God so loved the world that he gave his only Son,
> so that everyone who believes in him may not perish but
> may have eternal life."

Of course, we have to read this passage within its context in order to have a fair understanding of its meaning. It is clear from the context of this passage that it is the love of God that cost him his Son who died for the world. God (symbolically) consumed the sour taste of our hatred so that the world may experience God's love and compassion. God's mission was to save this world by his love and to continue to do so through his followers. David Watson in his book entitled *Accountable Discipleship*, states,

> "Discipleship meant following the commandments of
> Christ according to the law of love."

Love requires sacrifice and the cross, which is a symbol of our Christian faith, speaks to the reality of God's love for us. I have found it to be true in my life that without making sacrifices we are not able to offer genuine love toward others.

As a Parish we often talk about leadership and the kind of leadership that we want. I want to see a leadership which is able to face up to all the many challenges which our church faces today and not to run away from these challenges. This is what the Tongan *inu e fisi'inaua* concept is all about. For our Parish to have a future we need to be resilient, create a vision for growth, and also maintain our mission, which is to reach out to our world both now and in the future with the love of Christ.

Mālōlo: A Tongan Concept for Time-out

The value of renewal that comes from 'time out' – mālōlo.

Before I explore the implications of this Tongan word, *mālōlo*, let me define its meaning. According to C. Maxwell Churchward's dictionary of the Tongan language, the word *mālōlo* means "to rest, to die, be dead." These definitions are closely related to the notion of *time-out* in the contexts of sport and work. An English dictionary and thesaurus defines *time-out* as, "a suspension of play to rest, discuss tactics, a brief rest period."

Whenever I play with my two daughters and they become tired they put up their hands in a 'T' sign, by which they remind me that they need time-out. They need to have a break from the game as they can't continue, being too exhausted to play or keep up their concentration. I have seen that sign used in other sports when the referee stopped the game and allowed a player to have break or allowed the whole team to sit down with their coach and readdress their game plan.

The concept of *time-out* reminds us that we are vulnerable creatures. After a period of hard work or a hard game we deserve to have time-out, otherwise we would lose concentration and diminish the quality of our effort. The phrase *time-out*, then, is the equivalent of *mālōlo*, which is to rest or to have a break from hard work.

There are three aspects of the word *mālōlo* in the Tongan context I would like to emphasise, indicating the value of someone's hard work.

Firstly, *mālōlo* may refer to someone who died as the outcome of hard work. We use a phrase in the Tongan language for such a person, "*mālōlo pe mohe 'a e tangata ngaue*," meaning, "the resting or sleeping of a hard-working person." This phrase depicts the integrity and importance of the dead person, because of the quality of work that he offered for his community. Because he has given his best and his all, he deserves to have a sleep or a rest. He needs to have a time-out. Although the family will grieve for their loss it will be a healthy grieving, because they know that their loved one has done his best and now is at peace.

Secondly, *mālōlo* refers to someone who is going on vacation. Such a person has been working hard at the work place, and his employer has given him a long time-out from work to rest. Sometimes this person might go overseas to visit a friend, or just stay home and do gardening or house duties. While this person is on leave, he can reflect on his performance and at the same time regain energy before he starts back at work.

Thirdly, *mālōlo* refers to intervals during working hours for workers to have their morning tea, lunch and afternoon tea. Workers have the legal right to a work break in order to rest and to have refreshment. In doing so they regain the energy and concentration needed to be effective workers.

So the word *mālōlo* reminds us of the value of resting time. There is a time to work and a time to rest. The Book of Ecclesiastes, chapter 3, emphasises the uniqueness of every period of time.

> "For everything there is a season, and a time for every activity under heaven," says Ecclesiastes.

If work matters, then so does resting. We can't have one without the other. I believe we need both for they are both parts of God's creative order of which we are a part. William T. McConnell, in his book entitled *The Gift of Time*, states,

> "There is a scheduled rest, the seventh day, as a sign both of God's nature and of the complete rest which is ours to enjoy with our Creator." (p. 53)

I was fortunate to have a period of time-out when I was on annual leave, which is part of my work schedule every year. This time-out was not accidental, but planned according to the policy of the church and properly arranged with the Parish. My family and I enjoyed this time together at Owaka in the Catlins. Such a resting time allowed us to explore the beauty of the Catlins' natural environment. Each day was a pleasure because we were able to see and experience new things in nature. We enjoyed walking in the middle of the bush to see waterfalls and learn the names of our native trees. The beauty of the landscape and scenery attracted our attention and awareness. The song of the birds gave melody and harmony to our life every day. We could feel a sense of peace and comfort from each other's company. *Mālōlo* gave us this opportunity to reconnect with our family as well as to refresh ourselves for another year of service. There is a time to rest, and there is a time to work.

I would like to acknowledge the care and compassion of the Parish in giving me time-out *mālōlo* from work. I would like also to thank those who stepped in and took on my responsibilities while I was away from the parish. Without your concern for my wellbeing I wouldn't have had this opportunity. I believe everyone needs to have a break in order to function well in the work they do.

Jesus set the example when he went up the mountain with three of his disciples for a time of prayer and rest. During this time of rest, Jesus' face was transfigured, his energy was renewed, and his ministry was confirmed. I hope that we all have a chance to *mālōlo* when life is too busy and too stressful.

Tatali Pe, Tatali Pe: Waiting, Waiting

Waiting is a fact of life. Because waiting is uncomfortable
and uncertain, it requires patience, courage, hope
and trust.

Tatali pe, tatali pe is part of a Tongan love song. It is a song that was composed about a young man who was waiting for a long time for his lover to come. It seems that his lover was somewhere else. The longer he waited, the more frustration and worry he experienced. He did not know whether his lover would come at all and if she was coming, he did not know the time. Waiting can be an uncomfortable state for a person to be in, especially if waiting for a girlfriend or a boyfriend to come. Because waiting is uncomfortable and uncertain, it requires patience, courage, hope, and trust.

I remember arguing with my two daughters about putting up our Christmas tree at home. They wanted to put up the Christmas tree immediately on the first day of December. On that day we came home late at night and they wanted to put up the Christmas tree. I told them that we could put it up on the following day. They argued that we should put it up that night because we are in the month of December. I asked them this important question, "Can you wait until the following day?" They both replied, "No, we can't wait." They were both uncomfortable with the concept of waiting. For them, to wait is to increase their frustration and stress. Finally, they convinced me, and we put up the Christmas tree on that night. We put it up because of their persistence and determination. Is it possible to wait? Can we wait?

Waiting is part and parcel of expressing patience and displaying endurance. It emphasises the importance of time, and in particular the unknown time. We wait because either the time is not right, or the time is still to come. The concept of *time* is vital to the urgency of waiting. Because of the vitality of time we need to know the definition of *time*. There are two words in Greek that define the importance of time. These two words are *kairos* and *chronos*. *Kairos* is usually referred to as a fixed time and *chronos* usually refers to an unknown time. For instance, if we meet at 2pm then we have a fixed time and that is what *kairos* means. There is a fixed time for this meeting. However, if we arrange the meeting for next week and with no particular time, that's what *chronos* means. Waiting can be difficult when time is unknown and that is when *tatali pe* is required. *Tatali pe* doesn't give up on waiting, whether the time is known or unknown. The right time is God's timing, which requires an element of patience.

We are still in the Advent Season, which is a Season of waiting. We wait with worry, with frustration, with fear, with courage, with patience and with hope. Obviously, we have mixed feelings as we wait. How we feel will certainly affect the way we wait. There are lots of things that we are waiting for. While many island nations in the Pacific are worried about the rising of the sea levels, they are waiting with hope for the outcome of the Climate Change Summit in Paris. They are waiting with hope that the powerful nations will make decisions that will minimise global warming. While war and violence are increasing in many parts of the world, there are ongoing conversations about peace and reconciliation. Surely, communities and families affected by these wars are waiting with hope that peace will finally be achieved.

We heard two weeks ago from David Clark about the impact of poverty and lack of economic and social equality in our nation. He asked a question, "Can we be generous?" I am sure many families who live under the poverty line are waiting with hope that opportunities will come their way.

Waiting calls upon us to maintain our hope and trust in God who knows the unknown and what is best for us. The story in the Bible that reminds me of the importance of waiting is the story of Simeon in Luke 2:25–32. He was an old man who was waiting for the coming of Christ to liberate his people from their oppressors. His waiting was fulfilled when he saw baby Jesus. Then he was ready to pass away. He was waiting with hope and it was fulfilled in the person and the life of a baby. God worked in a mysterious and impossible way to complete Simeon's waiting.

I think the idea of waiting is real for us in our parish. We are waiting with fear, frustration, and worry because of the unknown future.

Tatali pe reminds us that despite an unknown future, and the length of waiting, we still need to be hopeful and faithful. We are hopeful because God – who knows the desires of hearts – will intervene and vindicate us. I wish you all a hopeful Advent as we wait for the birth of Christ.

Vahevahe: A Tongan Concept for Sharing Roles and Responsibilities in Ministry

*Ministry is not a one person band but a collective of
people who have the same passion and determination to
take risks in order to make a positive difference to people's
lives and communities.*

In the last two weeks I attended the Oceania Biblical Studies Association Conference in Samoa. It was an exciting event for all of us who participated, but especially for those who were in Samoa for the first time, like myself. The theme of the Conference was: Bible, Oratory and Oceania Literature. There were twenty presenters who presented papers from various contexts in Oceania on this theme. I was privileged to be one of the presenters who participated in sharing the rich heritage of our Pacific natural resources to extract ideas and concepts which can assist us in our interpretation of Biblical texts, and in transmitting and assimilating ideas through oral tradition and literature.

In my presentation, I used a Tongan word *vahevahe*, meaning, "sharing, dividing, or distributing" as a method to interpret Biblical texts, in particular the gospel of Matthew. I would like to use the same concept in this article in reference to ministry as a shared task, rather than just one person's responsibility.

Because ministry is a vast area and is also complex, I believe the concept of *vahevahe* is vital to its effectiveness and fulfilment. *Vahevahe* is a Tongan concept for sharing responsibilities and ideas for the purpose of lifting a burden and stress from someone or from a family. On important occasions such as funerals and weddings in the Tongan context, there are always attempts to share the costs and the responsibilities within the family/*kāinga* who is organising such an occasion. The main purpose of sharing the responsibilities and the costs is to ease the stress and burden this family/*kāinga* goes through. It is also for the purpose of allowing others to participate as way of empowering one another. Everyone who is involved in such occasions has the opportunity to give and receive, which demonstrates the value of sharing.

There are four ways that *vahevahe* could be viewed as a successful concept for ministry. Firstly, *vahevahe* is reciprocal, secondly, it is collaborative, thirdly, it is hospitable and fourthly, it is educational.

Reciprocity is an integral part of communal life. It enables everyone to give and to receive as a way to maintain mutual, intimate relationships. Because everyone participates in giving and receiving, it takes away pressure and stress. Being open to give as well as to receive is a vital part of *vahevahe*. You can't receive unless you are willing to give. This reciprocal attitude and practise would certainly create harmony among those who practice ministry. If there is a harmony in relationships, then hopefully ministry will run smoothly. It doesn't mean that everyone should agree with each other or practice the same ministry. However, it does mean that every ministry is different, and they need to exchange and share together. Paul uses the analogy of the human body in 1 Corinthians 12 as an example of reciprocity of gifts in ministry. Because every gift is unique, like the body's parts, they all need to be treated equally to give each of them equal opportunity for ministry.

Collaboration is always an expectation in ministry, especially in a community that is so diverse. It doesn't mean that everyone needs to agree with each other, but rather that everyone agrees to work together in the midst of their diversity and, if necessary, to agree to disagree.

I was impressed last Sunday with those who were flocking to the Forsyth Barr Stadium to support the World Peace Day. There were different groups from different faith communities, different ethnic groups and different dance groups. It was both their diversity and collaboration that contributed to the success of this event. It means that there was no single group that could claim the success of this event, but rather all the groups who were involved.

Collaboration is important to the success of ministry. We can't succeed with our purpose or goal in ministry unless we commit ourselves to work collaboratively. Therefore, we can't afford to compete against each other. We must empower each other to work together as a team. Henri Nouwen in his book, entitled, *Creative Ministry*, states,

> "Competition has become one of the most pervasive and also destructive aspects of modern education." (p.12)

Although, Nouwen's statement refers to the damage that competition causes in academia it can still apply to ministry. Those who are in ministry need to work collaboratively in the midst of their diversity, rather than trying to compete with each other.

Hospitality is very important in strengthening bonds in ministry. It is about sharing one's own resources to make someone else feel welcome and feel at home. In sharing resources with someone who is desperate, you not only detach yourself from your wealth of resources, but you also encourage the other person to do likewise. Real hospitality is not only one way, but two ways. The receiver of hospitality has something to give back as an expression of appreciation and thanks. It doesn't matter how big or small the act of hospitality is, so long as we are willing to share, which again denotes the concept of *vahevahe*. The exchanging of hospitality is not only about sharing resources but also valuing everyone's contribution.

Because the *vahevahe* concept is reciprocal, collaborative and hospitable, it is educational. The passing and sharing of resources among those who are doing ministry will extend knowledge and deepen understanding. It means that there is no end to learning in ministry.

Ministry is not a one person band but a collective of people who have the same passion and determination to take risks in order to make a positive difference to people's lives and communities. I hope that all members of our Parish will continue to be open to sharing our many gifts and resources together, for the improvement and growth of our ministry.

Easter Egg: A Symbol of life

Thinking about various things represented by Easter eggs.

Eggs have become icons for the Easter Season. Prior to Easter, we started to see Easter eggs in supermarkets and at The Warehouse. They are noticeable because they are right in the doorway as you enter. Nobody could miss seeing the Easter eggs and feeling the temptation to buy them. My two daughters love Easter eggs and every time we go to the supermarket, they want to buy them. They like Easter eggs because of their taste and their ability to nourish life. Easter eggs are not only for the purpose of consumption, but also for the purpose of creativity, which is a vital part of human life.

Before Easter, my two daughters were invited to join the students of the pre-school where my wife teaches for a school evening fun activity. This activity was called 'Easter Egg Hunting.' They started the evening with a pot-luck dinner and then the Easter egg hunting began. Prior to the activity, the staff of the pre-school were hiding Easter eggs around the school grounds for the students to hunt. Parents and families were standing around and watching while the students hunted for Easter eggs. I could see joy on the faces of those children who were able to find Easter eggs as quickly as they could, and also those who were able to find heaps. I could also see the disappointment on the faces of those who found few or no Easter eggs. The activity was simple and straight forward and the outcome was fun and educational. I am sure they all learned from this activity about fair competition and perseverance. They also learned about human interaction and sharing, which are unique parts of life.

Easter eggs can also symbolise protection and nurturing. They illustrate how the eggshell protects the chicks when a mother hen lays her eggs. Before the chicks come out to enjoy their environment, they have to be in the eggs first. The mother hen lays eggs for the new life to develop and grow. Within the eggs these new lives are nurtured and protected for 21 days before they are hatched. The hard shell of the egg becomes their shelter and security. We know that there is life in the eggs when they are hatched and the egg shells are left empty. The empty eggs prove that there is new life to continue on. We see the chicks under the wings of their mother hen, full of life and energy after leaving their egg shells. The egg shells gave them the opportunity to grow and develop. Eggs symbolise life.

When we look to the shape of an egg we see that it has an oval shape and it has no beginning or ending. There is nowhere on the egg that we can find a beginning or an end. This shape symbolises the never ending circle of life and love. The chick inside an egg experiences life and love everyday of its development.

Life and love represent something about God's attributes. God offers life everlasting and his love endures forever. This is the kind of message we gain from the Easter Season. Christ finally overcome hatred by his love, and defeated death by his resurrection life.

Easter eggs are used by various communities to represent new life and new beginnings. They symbolise the Easter Season and have an important theological meaning. We are told that the Christian customs relating to Easter eggs can be traced back as far as the early Christians of Mesopotamia, who stained eggs red in memory of the blood of Christ, shed at his crucifixion. Since this time the Christian Church has officially adopted this custom regarding the eggs as a symbol of the resurrection.

When we buy an Easter egg, we will find that it has an oval shape and is made of chocolate, sometimes with a hollow interior. This symbolises the empty tomb and the reality of resurrection life which we celebrate during Easter Season. This also reminds us about the message of the two angels who appeared to the women who first visited the body of Jesus. The angels said,

> "Why do you look for the living among the dead? He is not here, but has risen." (Luke 24:5b)

The stone which sealed the doorway has been opened and a new life has begun, for Jesus has risen from the dead. This is the good news that we celebrate on the first Sunday of Easter.

Because eggs symbolise the resurrection life, the Catholic church drafted a blessing to express the vitality of eggs for the Easter Season. This blessing was first recorded in 1610:

> "Lord, let the grace of your blessing come upon these eggs, that they be healthful food for your faithful who eat them in thanksgiving for the resurrection of our Lord Jesus Christ, who lives and reigns with you forever and ever."

As Easter eggs symbolise the start of a new life, so too can our lives start again during the Season of Easter. Our Parish needs a new beginning with the Risen Christ who can give hope to those who seek companionship and company. We are an Easter people and our role is to give hope to those who live under the shadow of death and misery. Let us continue to enjoy the taste of the Easter eggs and also share with each other the joy and love that we experience from them.

Peau 'o taimi: Knowing the Wave to Surf

*Reflections from a Pacific perspective on our
understanding of time and how the church should respond
to changing times.*

Recently, I walked down to St. Clair beach and saw surfers surfing in
the sea. I watched them with curiosity, observing how they surf and
when they surf. I noticed that the surfers congregate in the deep sea
waiting for the right wave to surf. Each one of them has their own
timing for the right wave and you can tell that by when they surf.
They are not all surfing at the same time, but surfing at different times
according to their knowledge of the right wave. I admire the surfers
for their skill and experience. Knowing the wave to surf signifies the
importance of time, i.e. good timing. The time has to be right in order
for a surfer to enjoy surfing as well as to reach the beach unharmed.
Those who do not know the correct wave to surf are likely to be in
danger and risk their lives. They could potentially drown or collide
into the rocks.

There is a time for every wave to roll down the beach and it is up to each
surfer to choose which one is suitable to catch. This understanding of
the waves' routine denotes the Tongan notion of *Peau 'o taimi* which
means, "waves of time." This notion *Peau 'o taimi* is different to the
Eurocentric concept of time. European understanding of time is
linear. It operates in a parallel line in a consecutive period. *Peau 'o
taimi* refers to the changes that constantly occur at certain times and
in different generations.

Tongans view the changes that take place as being like a spiral of
waves. They are inevitable and they come at different times with
diverse impacts upon the life of any society. These changes confront
traditions and customs that are the norms by which a society operates.
Changes that come at different times are like waves rolling down from
the deep ocean. They come unexpectedly, and it is up to individuals
to know how to adapt to them. Our failure and success depend upon
our knowing how to function in response to the inevitable changes

that we face. Just as surfers need to know which waves to surf, we, as Christians need to know the type of ministry which is appropriate for a time of change.

We need to know the signs of times in order to operate in a way that will be relevant and successful. Jim Davidson in his book, *Effective Time Management*, writes,

> "Time is an invaluable resource. When time is not utilized effectively, productivity and money are automatically lost. How you arrange your time is how you arrange your life and in your business, managing time is often synonymous with managing the job." (p. 7)

If we accept Davidson's concept of time as the appropriate way to respond to changes that happen, then we would have to control both the time, and the changes that occur.

However, that is impossible because change can happen at any time and in any context without our control. William T. McConnell in his book *The Gift of Time*, claims that time is understood differently in different cultural contexts. He argues that when we enter another culture, we have to readjust our understanding of time. He writes,

> "Whenever two different world or time views meet, there is need for an adjustment, a re-education on the part of all involved, in order for each to understand the thought patterns of the others." (p. 39)

This viewpoint is line with late Rev Dr Sione 'Amanaki Havea's interpretation of Pacific Time in his article entitled "Coconut Theology" in *South Pacific Theology*. He writes,

> "Many people when they are late talk about Fijian time or Tongan time, but the best suggestion is to call it the Coconut time, for it does not matter whether one is early or late. The important thing is that the task is done and the mission fulfilled." (p. 14)

While time is interpreted differently in different contexts, our role is to ensure that we take appropriate actions to meet the needs of the time and the change that occurs. Like a surfer who knows which wave to surf, we need to know the signs of the times and respond effectively. If we do not operate in ways that suit the needs of the time, we will fail our mission.

Our Presidential Team addressed the 2014 Methodist Conference with their theme, *A time to sow and a time to grow*. They claimed that in order for the Methodist Church to grow, its people need to know the type of gospel and message to proclaim to meet the needs of this generation. They reflected on the 200 years since Christianity came to New Zealand, when the gospel was first proclaimed by Reverend Samuel Marsden at Oihi in the Bay of Islands, on Christmas Day 1814. Since that day the gospel has been sown and has grown in many different parts of Aotearoa. Missionaries used different ways and tactics to meet the needs of that time and context. Surely, the methods that they used are no longer relevant in our era and generation. The church today has to reshape its ministry to meet the needs of this time and the context of this generation.

The closing of Broad Bay Methodist church was a challenge for this Parish. This closing provides an opportunity for our Parish and the whole Connexion to rethink our ministry in relation to our time and context. If we as a church do not understand the needs of the time and practice a ministry appropriate for our context, we will certainly fail. Like a surfer who knows which wave to surf, we should be a church which knows how to operate its ministry in a changing time.

Jesus valued the importance of time when he compared time to the cycle of nature. While he was teaching about the end of the age, he used the cycles of nature to illustrate the nearness of that time. He says,

> "Let the fig tree teach you a lesson. When its branches become green and tender and it starts putting out leaves, you know that summer is near. In the same way, when you see all these things, you will know that the time is near, ready to begin." (GNT, Matthew 24:32-33)

I believe that if this Parish is to enhance its life and ministry, we have to be flexible. We need to be open minded and responsive to the needs of our time and shape our ministry to fit our modern day context.

Taonakita: Every Life Matters

A Tongan perspective on the tragedy of youth suicide.

World Suicide Prevention Day St. Paul's Cathedral, Dunedin, 10 September 2014.

(This was part of my speech on this important occasion.)

Tena koutou, tena koutou, tena tatou katoa, Ta Lofa Lava, Ni Sabula Vinaka, Fakalofa lahi atu, Alohani, Malo e lelei, and warm Pacific greetings to all of you who are here tonight. I am glad to be invited to share my thoughts on this critical and important issue that has a devastating effect on our society. Suicide is becoming an epidemic that is unpredictable and unexpected. We are always surprised to hear that someone, maybe a close friend or a member of the family has committed suicide. Many questions start to arise for those who were close to this person, "How did it happen? Why didn't we see any sign? Why couldn't we stop it? What was the cause? Who should have noticed the signs?" These are questions that those who live ask as they continue to grieve for the death of a loved one or close friend who committed suicide.

During our first year in Dunedin, 2011, I experienced the destructive impact of suicide when one of my younger son's closest friends killed himself. It was a shock to my son, his family, his friends' families, to the school community and the wider community. This is something that this young person wasn't aware of when he decided to take his life. He never thought of the psychological and emotional damage that he would leave behind with his friends and his own family. Everyone who came in contact with him was affected in one way or the other because of his decision to take his own life. Almost at the same time, a few young Tongans committed suicide in various parts of Auckland. One of the suicides was committed inside one of the churches, which was a horrible situation. No one noticed any sign that these young people would take their own lives. Every life matters and we need to support it.

48

It is obvious that there are various causes of suicide and I am grateful to be here today to show my solidarity and support for the work that the Health sector and other agencies do, to prevent people from committing suicide. Suicide happens across ages, cultures, religions, communities and professions. Therefore, we need a co-operative effort to combat this epidemic in order to prevent or minimise it. I am glad that the Pacific communities are joining forces with other agencies to raise awareness and to help those who attempt suicide to seek help from the professionals.

One of the initiatives that the Pacific communities have started to deal with suicide is the formation of the national Pacific prevention programme, called FLO: Pasifika for Life. This programme is part of the Ministry of Health's suicide prevention Action Plan for 2013–16. Le Va is the national body that drives this initiative among the Pacific communities. Dr Monique Faleafa, the CEO of the Le Va says,

> "One of our recent actions was to create a booklet that talks about the top five tactics for helping to prevent Pasifika suicide."

She continues on to say,

> "Connecting with others is a tactic that Pasifika research shows works as a protective factor – vital for wellbeing, a sense of purpose and relationships with healthy flow. Connecting in a meaningful way with people near you today lets them know you care and that help is there when they need it."

The word for *suicide* in Tongan is *taonakita*. *Taonakita* is a combination of three words, of *tao*, *na* and *kita*. *Tao* means *spear*, *na* is an adjective and *kita* means *me* or *I*. Therefore, *taonakita* can literally mean, "I was killed by my own spear" or "I take my own life."

Taonakita is a taboo issue in the Tongan community and people rarely talk about it because of the *fakamā* (Māori *whakama*) or shame that it could impose on their families. Some Tongans see *tanokita* as a curse or some kind of evil spirit that possesses someone internally to hurt or take his/her own life. Internal hurt relates closely to the Tongan notion of *kafo e loto* (wounded heart). Obviously, a physical wound or an outward wound can be seen and can be treated, but a wounded heart is unseen, and it can be hard to find the appropriate treatment. Those who are in this situation feel powerless and hopeless. The easiest way for them to get rid of pain and hurt is to end their lives.

However, in order to break the taboo and to overcome the sense of *fakamā,* we need to build trust and respect. From a Tongan viewpoint, we can build trust and respect when the connection is strong through communal relationship and *kāinga/fanau (whanau)* bonds. People can talk freely when they are trusted and respected. I believe that this is what we need to encourage in our community. Our children need to know they are trusted by our willingness to listen to their voices.

Every life matters and it is God's will and purpose to create and nurture life and to allow a life to grow to it fullness. The scriptures speak highly about God as the Creator of life. Psalm 139 emphasises this nature of God when it mentions in verse 13,

> "For it was you who formed my inward parts;
> you knit me together in my mother's womb..."

I believe it is God's will to nurture and nourish every life, for every life matters.

I am both a Methodist minister and also a Tongan, which means I represent two communities in our *talanoa* this evening. *Talanoa* is the Tongan for "open conversation or talking." In talking we are able to pass on to others what our feelings and worries are and also at the same time, be able to listen to the voices and stories of others. Every story and voice is unique and worth listening to. May our voices join together tonight. Let us all be prepared to help our city and our communities. Tonight we are hearing many stories of the devastating effect of suicide and through those stories we can encourage others to feel trusted and respected to tell their own stories too.

Every life matters, and I believe we should join our voices and make every effort to prevent suicides from happening. Thank you for the opportunity to be part of the *talanoa* tonight. *Malo ʻaupito, leveleva e malanga kau tatau atu.*

Fofola e Fala: The Value of Connection

Connectedness brings self-esteem, healing and restoration.

Our parish celebrated recently the launch of a book edited by Ken Russell and Colin Gibson, entitled *Connections.*[4] The book comprises articles written by different authors, for different purposes and it is aimed at different readers. However, the main focus in all these articles is to make the connection between faith and the world we live in.

Ken Russell in the Preface interprets it more clearly as "...making connections between the life of the world and the gospel." This phrase highlights the value of connection. If we can't maintain the connection between the gospel and the world we live in, our message will certainly be out of context. Therefore, it is vital for the church to maintain its connection with the community where it exercises its ministry in order to be relevant. Keeping the connection is like building bridges that enable contact and communication from one end to the other. I realised this important aspect of connection during my recent visit to the United States of America.

My visit to the United States of America was for two reasons. Firstly, it was to officiate at the wedding of my niece, and secondly, to reaffirm my connection with my family in America. I arrived on 3 June at San Francisco Airport and my sister was waiting outside to pick me up. It took about one hour to get through the airport officials and to meet my sister. When I passed through the final checkpoint and walked out the gate, my sister was waiting to greet me. I was also able to greet my sister-in-law who came to pick up something that I brought for her. A little later my two nieces came to meet me.

The connection with my family in America started right at the airport. The words of welcome and greetings at the airport helped me to feel accepted and at home in this strange land. We drove from the airport to meet my two other sisters and their children. I was very pleased

---

4. *Connections: Celebration, Wisdom and Commentary from Dunedin Methodist Parish.* Edited by Ken Russell and Colin Gibson. Philip Garside Publishing Ltd, 2014.

to meet all of them again after seven years. Our meeting again shows the value of connection. Without connection we can easily become isolated.

Our reconnection denotes the Tongan concept of *Fofola e Fala* (unrolling the mat). *Fofola e fala* is a Tongan concept of bringing the family together for talking and dialogue. Unrolling of the mat is a role of the household head, which indicates to the rest of the kin that there is going to be a talk. Gathering together occurs when there is an important occasion about to happen in the family. It can also happen when there is reunion in the family to reaffirm relationships. This coming together is an opportunity to catch up with one another and to share ideas together. It would be impossible if the household was scattered and divided. *Fofola e fala* is an open forum that gives everyone in the household the freedom to join in and share ideas. If those who sit on the unrolled mat are hindered from speaking, then the spirit of *Fofola e fala* is violated. *Fofola e fala* is a fair way of making everyone in the household feel included and valued. Those who are present on such occasions treasure a valuable time of connectedness in the household.

However, despite the joy of joining others on the unrolled mat it might not be possible for everyone to have a space, especially when there are many people who want to sit on the mat! It is quite easy to forget or avoid the weak members of the household in a conversation or dialogue. This is a reality for children and women in the context of *Fofola e fala*. Women and children are occasionally sidelined because they are seen as ignorant or lacking in experience. They are assumed to be too narrow minded to take part in a conversation or consultation. This kind of belittling attitude is widely embedded across various cultural contexts.

I realised this fact on my visit to one of the local churches in America where the homeless were welcomed and given meals. I don't know the causes of their homelessness, but they came from various backgrounds with different problems. The majority of them have no place to live because they are disconnected from the community and their families. The impact of disconnection had a huge influence upon them in terms of their self-value and self-esteem. I wondered at that stage, just how many people are like these homeless people in America, and the rest of the world.

Last Sunday many churches commemorated Refugee Sunday. It was a Sunday to remember refugees and the reasons they become refugees. These people have been displaced from their homes and families either because of war or natural disaster. They moved from their communities because they have been forced to move. Christian World Service sent us materials for Refugee Sunday. They mentioned that about 11 million people in the world are refugees. This is an appalling figure. These are all people who are longing for connection and contact. Unless we have the will to give space for everyone to live, we will not be able to avoid a further increase in the number of refugees.

Our Christian tradition, and the charter of compassion hanging on the wall of the Mornington Methodist Church hall in Dunedin, remind us of our role to offer hospitality to these people. It is through the offering of space for the refugees and the homeless, that we are able to help them to reconnect to the community. I am glad that New Zealand is one of those nations that is prepared to offer such a space for refugees. Offering of space articulates the value of connection. I believe that working intentionally for connection, has an integral part to play in the realm of God.

The Season of Pentecost, which we celebrated a few Sundays ago, demonstrates the nature of God in connection with creation. In the Spirit, God is present in the creation of the world, giving the world life as mentioned in the two creation stories in the Book of Genesis. It was the Spirit of God who breathed life into the creation, together with the first human being. The same Spirit breathed life into the early followers of Christ, giving them strength for their mission. I believe it is the same Holy Spirit (*Laumalie Ma'oni'oni*) who is present in our lives to empower us in our ministry and connect us with God and with one another. I am doing my best to live in connection with God, with other people and with our world. How can we all best help those who are longing for connection to do so in a way which will bring them healing and restoration?

Omarama with Love

*Holiday experiences heighten awareness of love,
community and the natural world.*

Our family holiday in Omarama was truly an experience of love. Our holiday connected well with the meaning of the name *Omarama*, which is *Place of light*. Love is really enlightening and empowering, as is light. We experienced love ourselves and from others during our time in Omarama. These experiences renewed our love for each other, for other people and for the natural world.

We arrived in Omarama on 12 January, which was a Sunday. It was very quiet and the weather was overcast. We arrived safely at the Omarama Holiday Park and went straight to pick up the key to our cabin. The girls were excited with our cabin, especially having a bunk bed. However, that excitement was only short lived when they started to quarrel and argue about who is going to sleep on the top of the bunk bed. I immediately intervened trying to resolve this conflict situation but with no success. At the end we thought that to satisfy them, they would both have to sleep on the top of the bunk. Although, it might be a risky option it became a successful one! As the nights were in progress the girls started to learn slowly how to share and allow the other person to take that space. This is the kind of experience that our girls learned. They learned to love each other in the midst of their disagreement. Perhaps, they started to realize that love has a cost.

We arrived in Omarama in the evening and I could see everyone in the Holiday Park was ready for dinner. The facilities in the Holiday Park are for everyone to share. There is only one kitchen, one bathroom and toilet for everyone to share. Families and individuals are obliged to share these facilities and it was really an amazing experience. We were quick to learn how to work together in a community of different people. The dynamics were wonderful. Fathers and mothers, wives and husbands, friends, boys and girls all worked together. There was no conflict or dispute among families or individuals in the sharing of the facilities. Everyone was willing to share and to give space. Although, we did not know each other there was still a common concern in this community for the wellbeing of each other. Both mothers and fathers were cooking for their families, and children were helping by washing their dishes. Families shared their food with other families. Our family adapted quickly to the life of this community. It required us to reinterpret and restructure the way we understand roles and responsibilities in the Tongan culture.

This attempt to learn new way of doing things fits in well with our family's situation. When we arrived at Omarama, my wife, Naomi had a stomach bug, which caused her to vomit and feel nauseous. It meant that I would be the only one in our family was fit to do the cooking and dish washing. This responsibility lasted for four days of our one week holiday. I did the cooking and also the dish washing, which gave Naomi time to enjoy the holiday fully. Certainly, it meant I did not get such a good holiday. However, this experience prompted me to realise the importance of sharing responsibilities, which affirm our mutual love and respect for each other. Omarama gave us that realisation of the significance of it for our relationship. Perhaps, that was a fulfillment of the advice that I had from one of the women of our church who told me that Naomi deserves to have a rest and for me to do the cooking during the holiday! It was a dream come true for that person!

The purpose of our holiday was not only to relax and renew strength so that when we came back to work we felt renewed and fresh. For me the purpose of our family holiday was more than that. One of the purposes of our holiday was to explore the natural world. Because of my wife's sickness we were not able straight away to fulfil that wish. We had to wait until Naomi recovered. It was a long wait and I thought that we couldn't fulfil our original plan. However, after three days of waiting Naomi recovered and was then able to travel to distance places. On the fourth day our dream came true. We woke up in the morning and had breakfast and then prepared our lunch and drink for our adventure.

It was truly a fine day. The sun was shining and the sky was clear. Our plan for this day of adventure was certainly enjoyable and exciting because of the wonderful weather. We planned to drive to Mt Cook to view and experience the beauty of those mountain ranges but we did not make it to Mt Cook. There were some health issues of our passengers and we couldn't travel that far.

However, no one was moaning about the fact that we couldn't visit all the sites we would have loved to visit. Wherever we visited on this one day, we took great pleasure in the natural beauty of our surroundings. On our way to Lake Ohau we started to realise our lack of experience in that region. We thought that we are so lucky to live in this land that is peaceful and to have the chance to explore its environment. It really opened our eyes to see the splendour and wonder of God's creation. When we left Omarama, driving to Lake Ohau we immediately encountered the magnificence of the Waitaki Valley.

The route we travelled, the desert we drove past, the hills that surrounded us, the valleys, the mountains, the rivers, the lakes and the native birds opened our eyes to new ways of understanding the creation. These marvellous dynamics gave us the impression that if we love and care for this natural world, its beauty will continue to be maintained. When we arrived at Lake Ohau, our destination, we stopped and had a picnic there. The girls courageously bathed in the shallow part of the lake, while Naomi and I took pleasure in the peaceful environment. It was really a day of great adventure for our family. We came home after our family holiday with renewed love in our family, for our diverse community, and also for our natural world. We also returned home with a deeper love for God who guided and protected us throughout this marvellous voyage. It is through these experiences that we will always remember Omarama with love.

Pacific Perspective

Inspiration for young people from the Pacific.

Recently I was invited to do the opening prayer in an inter-school speech contest on "Pacific Perspective" at Otago Girls High School on Thursday, 15 August 2013 at 6.30pm. This was an historical event because it was the first of its kind held in Dunedin. Because of the nature of the evening and the purpose of this event, I asked the organisers if I could say something important before I offered the prayer. I told them when I was invited to come forward that I am not coming only to say a prayer and then go home. I want to contribute to the significance of this event to the Pacific Community here in Dunedin.

So, here is an extract from a speech that I made before I continued on with a prayer.

> Tena koutou, tena koutou, tena tatou katoa, Ta Lofa Lava, Bula Vinaka, Kia orana, Fakalofa Lahi atu, Taloha ni, Malo e lelei and warm Pacific greetings. It is indeed an honour and privilege to take part is this evening on this unique occasion for the Pacific students in Dunedin. My name is Siosifa Pole and I am from the Pacific. I was born in Tonga in the village of Fua'amotu, where Tonga International airport is located. When I grew up and did all my primary and high school education in Tonga, I was constantly told that Tonga is a dot in the world map. It is hard to recognise by those who have eye sight problems. Yes, we are a small island as are other islands in the Pacific, compared with the powerful nations in the world. This aspect of smallness disempowered me immediately and reduced my striving for educational success. I realised that I did not have the resources and facilities that could assist me to excel in my education.

However, it is the perspective of one of our Pacific renowned scholars, the late Professor Epeli Hau'ofa, a Tongan anthropologist, who inspired and motivated me with his article, entitled *Sea of Islands*. In this article, he claims that we are not only islands, but islands in the sea. We live both in the islands and also in the sea. Both the islands and the sea are instrumental in resourcing and nurturing our people in the Pacific. Therefore, if we add together the landscape, the underground and the Pacific Ocean, which is ours, our island nations in the Pacific are obviously bigger than the most powerful nations in the world! Perhaps tonight, on this Pacific Perspective Evening, we need to think big and beyond our smallness. We need to stretch our minds like an eagle's wings and fly above our limitations.

I read a book written by the Franks brothers, who are also All Blacks. It is an inspiring book for young people who strive for success in any field of their interest. They write in this book this unique phrase, "We are all born to be equal but some work harder during pre-season than others." Although, they wrote from a rugby perspective it can apply to any area of life. Indeed, God created each of us to be equal but what that means to you and to me will make the difference in our lives. Don't let what others think of you diminish or discourage you in relation to your dreams to succeed in your studies and also your seeking a career for the future. May God bless you all on this historic occasion."

This is the end of my short speech but I continued on with a prayer before the MC came forward and called each contestant to share their speech. It was a long night but I was impressed with the speeches of these young students. I am sure all of us who were present were challenged and inspired.

All the speakers on that evening were of Pacific descent and I felt that my introduction set the platform for each of them to build their speeches on. It was not planned to be that way but it did happen, which was impressive. Although we came from different families and cultural backgrounds we all had something in common, i.e. our Pacificness and our smallness. We were trying that evening to encourage one another to come out of that cocoon and realise that opportunities are out there for them to grasp. They have the potential and the ability to grow big and think big.

A couple of Sundays ago I was impressed by a photo in our bulletin of Celia Cannon, Rachel Jones and Joy Clark with a title on the top, *The Power of One*. The title on this photo was referring to Celia Cannon as the only child in the children's talk and also in the Sunday School on that day. It was certainly powerful because Celia was able to draw the attention of the whole congregation to herself as a unique member of our church family.

In the gospels, Jesus compares the Kingdom of God to a mustard seed, the smallest of all the seeds. He also compares the Kingdom of God to children, the most vulnerable people in our society. He valued the giving of the poor widow, although her offering was small when compared to the rich people. Why was smallness important to Jesus? What is it that smallness can offer? Should we value smallness?

Everything that grows big started small and that's why smallness is important. While anything or anyone is still small they require special attention and careful consideration. This Sunday is Father's Day and we celebrate the significance of father's roles in families and homes. From a Tongan perspective, a father's role is to provide for his family's sustenance and security. The growth and the health of the vulnerable members of the family are dependent on his compassion to nurture and cherish their lives. He has to ensure that the weak members of the family are secure and safe. I suppose this is a general expectation of all fathers in any community, to consider the importance and the uniqueness of the small ones. We can apply the same principle to other areas in our community and our role to protect the vulnerable ones and to hear to their voices. By listening to their voices and considering their points of view, we will enable them to grow beyond their set boundaries and their current limitations.

The Creation Story from a Tongan perspective

Learning truth from different stories of creation.

I read recently a small booklet written by Keith Rowe, entitled *Charles Darwin – Secular Saint*. In that booklet, Keith Rowe suggests that Christians should value the contribution of scientists in our search for truth. He claimed that Charles Darwin was one of those scientists who opened a new way of understanding and thinking about creation. He was among the first to suggest that life had evolved as a natural process without the interference of an all-powerful, controlling deity. Charles Darwin's book *On The Origin of Species* was controversial in the life of the church in the 19th century, but it brought another dimension to our understanding of the creation story.

I suppose we all have that instinct of constantly looking for the truth. We continue to explore until we find the truth about God and his creation. As a Tongan, I have my own story of creation, which I would like to share with you. In this story you will see that the creation of the human race was a combination of a deity's involvement and also a process of evolution. This story can be called *The Tongan Legend of the Creation of the First Human Beings*. It is translated from a book written in the Tongan language by Masiu Moala, entitled, *'Efinanga*. This is the version of the creation story from a Tongan perspective.

> The whole land was covered with green vegetation. Tangaloa Tufunga (god of the sky) told Tangaloa 'Atulongolongo (god of the land) to wander around and to look for the island of 'Ata (one of the islands in the eastern side of Tongatapu, the main Island) for there is a big *fue* (a type of creeper plant) which grows there. Tangaloa 'Atulongolongo asked Tangaloa Tufunga what he would do if he found the *fue* plant?
>
> Tangaloa Tufunga responded, "You cut off one of the branches, and leave it there to rot. Out of that rotten branch of the *fue* plant would come a huge *'uanga* (worm)

and you have to cut it into three pieces. From them, three living persons will come out and you will name them, *Kohai* (What), *Koau* (I am), and *Momo* (Crumb)." These are the first human beings who were created, multiplied and scattered on the land, who became the origin of the Tongan people.

There are significant aspects that come out of this story, which are; the involvement of a deity in the creation, and also the evolution of one species to create other species. This process of creation has a combination of pain and also of new life. A branch was cut from the *fue* plant and left to rot. Out of that a new life began of a big worm. That new life was cut into three pieces and out of these three pieces came three human beings. Life cannot remain the same, for it evolves and certainly there is a connection with Darwin's theory of evolution.

We have in Genesis chapters 1 and 2, different versions of another creation story. It is a story that was told from a Hebrew perspective.

This story starts with God who created the universe (cosmos) from nothing (ex nihilo) by his words. He brought life out from chaos and from disorder, bought order. Every day God created certain things according to his plan and he saw each one of them was very good. He created the first human being from the dust of the earth in his image and he called him Adam. He put Adam into a deep sleep and took out one of his rips and created a woman, and Adam named her Eve. A deity was in control in this creation story and the whole purpose was to bring harmony and order into the creation.

This harmony was short-lived when Adam and Eve abused their power to look after God's creation with love and care. They had been given the power to be good stewards of God's creation but they violated that right for their own personal gain. Their action resulted in their being expelled from the Garden of Eden. Adam and Eve gave birth to their children, which resulted in the growth of the human race. Life cannot stay the same, for it evolves, develops and grows.

Those two creation accounts prove to us that there was a deity involved in the creation of our world and that life cannot stay the same, for it evolves. Change, development and progress are parts of the created world we live in. We are created to be part of this global household. Life is like a journey, filled with surprises, pleasures and tragedy. Through that journey we evolve and are transformed by the contexts of where we live. These changes can be for good or for ill.

Last Sunday was World Refugee Sunday, a reminder for us of our responsibility in this global household toward refugees and those who have no place to live. People have fled their homes and countries in fear for their lives. Wars, persecution, oppression, and prejudice have forced people to move away from the places that God created for them to live and enjoy life.

I believe that when we divorce God from the world, we act in an ungodly manner toward our fellow human beings. But when we see that God is within creation and takes part in the evolution process, we will understand that we have a responsibility toward our fellow human beings and the rest of the creation. The Creator God calls us to treat each other with love, care, respect and compassion. God created us in his own image and would love to see us treating each other, and whole of creation, in the same way that he treats each of us. Although changes are inevitable, we have a mission to see others as people who are created in the image of God, who loves us all.

Femolimoli'i & Fetoliaki:
Reciprocity: a Way for Survival

Thoughts about the impact of inequality upon society.

I have read a thought-provoking and informative book entitled, *The Spirit Level,* by Richard Wilkinson and Kate Pickett. The authors deal with the impact of inequality upon society and its people. They look at how inequality affects health, environment, crime, human behaviour and the status of individuals. The authors claim at the end of the book that in order for society to be healthier, more economically sustainable, with less crime, and peaceful, there should be equality.

The authors write,

> "Modern societies will depend increasingly on being creative, adaptable, inventive, well-informed and flexible communities, able to respond generously to each other and to needs wherever they arise. Those are characteristics not of societies in hock to the rich, in which people are driven by status, insecurities, but populations used to working together and respecting each other as equals." (p. 263)

Both writers argued that if we work together to address inequality in our community we can resolve some of our social problems. But can we be equal? Can everyone be equal? How do we see and understand equality?

Equality for me as a Tongan is about reciprocity. Reciprocity is defined by the dictionary as, "to give and receive." In order for equality to exist there should be a desire to give and to receive. Those who have more than they need must have a generous heart to give, and that the same is expected of the recipients. They are expecting to give back whatever they can offer as part of their commitment to equality. They receive freely and so they have to give back freely.

There are two Tongan words that identify the meaning of reciprocity in a Tongan context, which are; *femolimoli'i* and *fetoliaki*. *Femolimoli'i* means, "to share your smallness" and *Fetoliaki* means, "To lift one's burden." On one hand *femolimoli'i* denotes the reality that we don't have or know everything. Therefore, we need to want to receive as well as to give. On the other hand, *fetoliaki* refers to the willingness to share someone's burden. Because everyone has burdens it is therefore the responsibility of everyone to help share each other's burden. Both words explicate the understanding of reciprocity. The important thing about giving is not the quantity but the quality of the giving.

What matters is not how big or how small your gift is but the heart that goes with the giving. Every gift or contribution, even a very small one, will have a positive impact on someone's need, and that is what *femolimoli'i* means. The same will happen to a person's burden, whether a financial burden or a health burden. It will be lifted when there is a willingness to share and that is what *fetoliaki* means.

John Wesley advised his followers about the significance of giving as a way to minimize inequality in his society. In a letter he wrote in 1770, he writes,

> "The dangers of prosperity are great... if poverty contracts and depresses the mind, riches sap its fortitude, destroy its vigour, and nourish its caprices."

In his sermon on the subject of wealth he emphasised three main points,

> "Gain all you can! Save all you can! Give all you can."

John Wesley believed that by giving and sharing we can relieve someone's poverty. We, the Methodists of today, are the inheritors of this tradition. We are not only giving financially but we also give our time, our energy, our intellectual activity, our gifts of ministries, and our love for others. We are not only receiving, but are also at the same time giving. Because we do not have or know everything, we are challenged to humble ourselves and open our minds both to receive and to give. It is through reciprocal responses that we can deal with inequality in our society as well as in our church.

Our parish is currently dealing with many issues that involve equality and inequality. The fact of the matter is that we cannot all be equal, and we will never be equal in every way, but we can help and share with each other to minimise the inequalities in our Parish.

One of the issues that we currently deal with in our parish is the assessment of our church buildings. Obviously, we will try our best to deal with this issue equally, but this will not be easy. Some of our congregations are better resourced than others in terms of finances and membership, while others are struggling because of the lack of resources. While we are different in many ways we are called to share the burden with others in our parish. As Christians, we will find it easier to share if we proceed with a spirit of reciprocity.

Reciprocity is not really about the quantity but about the quality. It is the quality of our giving and sharing that can make a difference in someone's life. *Femolimoli'i* and *fetoliaki* could be two values that shape an authentic reciprocity. Furthermore, an authentic reciprocity is only possible with a heart of love. Love is at the heart of the gospel and that is where reciprocity should be based. Paul in 1 Corinthians 13 emphasises love as the most important of all the spiritual gifts. He suggests that if we do anything without love than we would be like a noisy gong or a clanging cymbal.

People survive when the powerful have the will to share with the powerless in love, when the rich share with the poor in love, when the stronger give to the weaker in love, and when we all have a common bond of giving and receiving from each other in love. I believe when we do not have the will to do this, then the quality of our parish life together, will be at risk. Reciprocity is a pathway for survival.

The Reefs of Today Will Become the Islands of Tomorrow

A Tongan concept of valuing children.

Tonga is made up of 176 islands and only 26 of them are inhabited. Some of these islands are volcanic and others are made out of coral reefs. Volcanic islands rise above sea level. However, islands that are made out of coral reefs face the dangers posed by rising sea levels. Despite this threat, people have lived in these islands for thousands of years. These islands have become their home and their inheritance. Furthermore, their roots and their identity are formed in these islands. They travel and migrate overseas but they always think of these islands as their home. Life began and was nurtured in those islands that are made out of coral reefs.

Coral reefs are formed by small sea animals (coral polyps) that live in colonies. Hard corals formed the coral reefs with their limestone skeletons. Amazingly, they do this with the help of tiny, microscopic plants that actually live inside them. These coral reefs eventually evolve over millions of years to create coral islands, like many of the islands of Tonga, including the island of Tongatapu where I came from. These coral inhabited islands give the people of Tonga a land to live on and to cultivate for their sustenance. The land they live on was not able to form without a long period of nurturing and protection. It took a considerable amount of time and care for these coral reefs to evolve into these islands. Generations have been benefiting from the produce of these islands. The reefs of today will become the islands of tomorrow.

The development of reefs into islands symbolises the Tongan concept of child rearing. Children are like reefs that are untouched and innocent in their natural environment. Yet they are vulnerable, like the reefs, to exploitation and abuse. They expect to be looked after and nurtured to grow physically, mentally and spiritually healthy, for the future of families. The nation depends on them.

Children are the treasure of the nation and if they are not protected, the cost to the community will be great. If we want a nation that has a hope for the future we need to look after the children of today. We can't afford to wait at the bottom of the cliff with an ambulance to heal their wounds and mend their scars. We need to act now before is too late.

During the Annual Conference of the Methodist Church, the President and Vice-president launched the Connexional theme for the next ten years, which is, "Let the children live." How can we implement this vision? What are our strategies to address this important issue? Where could we find the resources to handle this issue? Do we have the energy to do it? We might have different responses to these questions, but the bottom line is that we must act now before is too late.

The Commissioner for Children reported to Conference that 25% or 270,000 of the children in New Zealand are living in poverty. Surely, there will be life-long consequences for children's health, education and well-being, which will in turn have an impact on the security, economy and welfare of this land. Government policy that doesn't help to ease the problems of poor and low income families, will affect the wellbeing of their children. Child Poverty Action Group[5] reported in 2012,

> "New Zealand's most vulnerable children are bearing the brunt of the Government's punitive sanctions against beneficiaries, with solo parents making up the majority of those with children having their benefits cut."

If the reefs of today are to be the islands of tomorrow, and if the children of today are to be the leaders of the future, then surely the government, and the whole of New Zealand society, have a responsibility to nurture and care for their personal development.

As I am writing this article, there is a case in the court of a man accused of killing his stepchild. Child abuse and violence against children is an appalling social issue in New Zealand. I believe it is

---

5. https://www.cpag.org.nz/

a side effect of poverty. Children who grow up in families who live under the poverty line are likely to go through tough times.

Let the children live should not only be the theme of the Methodist Church, but a theme for every parent in this land of Aotearoa New Zealand to ponder, because it is God's will that all children should live. Psalm 127 verse 3 says,

> "Behold, children are a heritage from the LORD,
> The fruit of the womb is a reward." (NKJV)

Children are portrayed in this verse as a heritage and reward from God, which are important metaphors for our future survival. We can't afford to lose our heritage and our fruit. If we lose both of them, then there is not much hope for our future.

In a Tongan context, those who do not have their heritage, namely the land, have no hope for their future. We are depending on the land for cultivation and for accommodation. The land was formed through careful nurturing of the reefs of the past. Thus, our mission is to look after the reefs of today, for one day they will form an island, which will provide land for people to live and cultivate for their welfare. Similarly, we are called to invest in our children today for they are the future of families, of the nation and of the church.

Feau: A Tongan Concept of Comfort
for a Grieving Family

A Tongan perspective on the grieving process.

I am pondering this concept of comfort during a time of grief for many losses, because of my experience of many deaths in the parish this year, and also the death of my wife's youngest sister in the last two weeks. It is through the support of many people that our grieving family feel comforted. This feeling of comfort and encouragement denotes the notion of *feau* as a Tongan concept for peace during a time of a death.

Feau has a lot of meanings from a Tongan perspective. There is no one single English word that can capture the whole meaning of this word. In general terms *feau* is used as a noun and it refers to "wholeness" or "self-sufficiency." It reflects an experience of someone who is in their comfort zone. There is nothing to worry about, for everything is provided. However, in a funeral context, *feau* is used as a verb. It is a term that describes all the actions that have been taken before, during and after a funeral in order to bring healing and wholeness to the grieving family.

There are various terms in the English language that depict the meaning of *feau* in the Tongan context. These terms are; to comfort, to grieve with, to mourn and to weep with, to share the load with and to share responsibilities with. It seems that all of these terms in one way or the other exhibit the nature of *feau* in the Tongan funeral, which gives comfort to the grieving family.

Because *feau* in the context of funeral is a verb, it could refer to every action that everyone offers to support a family during their time of sorrow because of a death of a loved one. *Feau* is not a once and for all action, but is a process that involves everybody. One of the obvious expressions of this process in a funeral is the actual participation. Any participation, in any capacity at a funeral gives comfort and encouragement to the grieving family.

Here are some of the ways people get involved in the process of *feau*; contributing food, providing financial assistance, serving the visiting families and friends, taking part in cooking and providing food for visiting people. When I was in Tonga I saw people every day come with food, people who helped in cooking, those who were willing to offer financial assistance, and those who provided hospitality to the visiting guests. These actions demonstrated communal participation as a strength of the Tongan community, in order to ease the sorrow of the grieving family in their time of loss.

Being present at a funeral is a vital part of the *feau* process. Without being present there is no comfort. From a Tongan viewpoint, the more people who come to your funeral, the more comfort you may experience. It may cost a lot for a grieving family to feed a multitude of people coming to a funeral, but it cannot be compared to the peace and encouragement that they receive from them. Concerned and caring people may come and go for five to ten days and they may put pressure on the grieving family's resources, but their presence affirms the support of the wider community. It reminds the grieving family that they are not alone in their sadness and sorrow. There are people who care enough to share with them by being present with them in their time of need. These people usually come with stories about their relationship with the dead person to share with the family. As they share their stories they bring all to life the memories of the past, which connect the family and their loved one. This conversation and sharing comforts the family in the midst of their despair.

In the process of *feau*, the significance of time for Tongans is not the same as for Europeans. On the one hand, Europeans view time as something to be restricted and fixed. On the other hand, Tongans view time as something that is flexible. What matters is not when you start or end any task, but when it is completed. Taking time to be with a grieving family is, in the eyes of the Tongans, very important for their wellbeing during the mourning period. Those who go and spend time with the grieving family usually stay for long hours, days, or even weeks to offer support. This is what those who have a close relationship with the grieving family, either a blood or friendship relationship, do to support them.

The church plays a vital role in providing pastoral care during the mourning period. It is a normal expectation for the minister and the whole church to be present to pray with the grieving family for days before the end of the mourning period. The mourning period is the three days after the burial. Spending time with the grieving family helps them to cope with their grief in a positive way. In the short time I was in Tonga, the minister and the church offered prayers and sang hymns and Christian songs with the grieving family, every evening during the three days of mourning. This support certainly helped the husband of the woman who died and their children to cope with the loss of a loved one who was so dear to them.

Feau is a Tongan concept of comforting a family who have experienced the loss of a loved one. I am sure this concept can apply to any culture and any context. The three aspects of action, being present and spending time, are important parts of the role of those who offer care and support during any kind of loss.

These aspects can apply to other contexts. The action of our friends and families, your willingness to be present and to spend time with us, gave us comfort in our loss. These actions of kindness remind me of the words of the prophet Isaiah to a people who had lost everything except their God.

> "Comfort, O comfort my people, says your God."
> *Isaiah 40:1*

Feau cannot be completed until God is involved, and I believe that it is through your thoughtful prayers that God gave Naomi and the family comfort during this time of mourning. Thank you for your action, for your presence and your spending time with us in our sorrow.

Tauhi-va: Oceania: A Concept of Sacred Space

Reflections on our place and God's place.

I always enjoy walking down St. Clair beach. On the beach, I constantly meet surfers who are surfing in the sea and Life Savers, people who practise rescuing people who are in trouble in the sea. I also meet with people who love to come and have meals at The Esplanade and other restaurants at the beach while they are enjoying the view of the deep ocean. When I sit down and look at the deep ocean I cannot see anything else apart from an open space. As I look with anticipation, I slowly realise that this is not merely a space, but a sacred space. This space has a meaning and a purpose for the whole of the created order, as well as the creation of Oceania and the Pacific Ocean as a special place for us.

Oceania is created out of sea and land. However, the area of the sea is much bigger than the total area of the land in Oceania. The sea in Oceania is known as the Pacific Ocean, where all the island nations of Oceania are scattered. There are 20,000 to 30,000 islands that spread out in the 165 million square kilometres of the Pacific Ocean. These island nations are not connected. The sea divides them and gives them space to enjoy their individual autonomy.

Aotearoa New Zealand is one of those lands that is wonderfully situated in the southern part of the Pacific Ocean. It is the sea space that gives the inhabitants of Aotearoa freedom to live the way they like to without interference. The sea creates a sacred space to celebrate individual uniqueness. Yet, the sea is also a means of connecting these island nations. Although they are not connected by land, the sea connects them, for it reaches to each island's shore and beaches. Moreover, the ocean is a sacred space of connection.

As I looked to the deep sea with astonishment, I was reminded of the crucial value of space in human relationships. In Tongan culture, *space* is very important for any mutual relationship. This space is known in Tongan language as *Va*. It is a liminal space between two or more people who have a mutual relationship. The *Va* is a space in between that has to be kept in order for harmony and peace in the relationship to be maintained. Respecting that between space is known in Tongan as *Tauhi-va* (keeping the 'in-between' space). Retaining such a space is a well-known concept across the Pacific island nations. The sacredness of that space reminds everyone to treat it with respect. It gives each person the luxury of claiming individual uniqueness in a community.

If the space in-between is exploited then there will be damage to the relationship. Furthermore, there will certainly be a violation of individual rights. We have witnessed the damage that has been done by those who have no respect for the space in-between places or between people. They forced themselves to cross over that liminal space without any consultation or dialogue, and the outcome is horrendous. One example that came to mind is the 'War against Terror.' This war was born out of those who violated the sacredness of space between peoples and nations. Thousands of lives and millions of dollars were wasted because of the violation of in-between space.

If the space in-between has to be shared, then there should be a point of negotiation and agreement. Everyone has to be informed and consulted. Doing so will create a sense of respect and compassion toward one another.

The presidential team's address at the 99th Conference of the Methodist Church of New Zealand, held in Auckland last month, was titled, "Our place – God's place." The main emphasis of their address was the significance of having a place for everyone and for God. Our place is God's place and that is what connects us. The Ocean can be used as a metaphor for God's love and God's presence among us. If God is big like the Ocean space, then that is our point of connection. Although we may be scattered as individual people, it is God's love that connects us all. It is the ocean of his love that reaches equally to everyone with grace and hope. No one can exploit that space because everyone has equal access to that sacred space. Our place is God's place and God's place is our place too. Therefore, we can't distance ourselves from one another; we are accountable for the welfare of everyone, for we are all in God's place.

I believe this notion of the ocean as a space of connection has important implications for ministry in the Methodist Church of New Zealand. If our church is true to its theology and philosophy of connexionalism, then we must value everyone's contribution and treat everyone with respect. It means that we must listen with open eyes, ears and hearts to every voice and concern. We might not agree on everything but we can dialogue and negotiate, and that is the real nature of in-between/ocean space. Therefore, the ocean reminds us of the sacredness of human relationships, our relationship with the created order and with God. Our role is to ensure that those relationships are treated with respect and appreciation.

Rock Can't but Sand Can:
an Oceanic Approach for Unity

*Thinking about new metaphors for Gods unconditional
love, inclusiveness and unity.*

I am writing this article with due respect to the Tangata Whenua
(people of the land) and also to those who later resided in the land,
the Manuhiri (the settlers), and do not intend to cross over any
boundary or violate anyone's privacy. As a native of Oceania, it is a
right protocol to acknowledge the presence of the people who first
inhabited this place, where I am working and practising my ministry.
Their efforts laid the foundation on which I begin my ministry. It
is indeed an honour to be asked to contribute to this column of the
Connection. There is a Tongan saying, *potopoto a niu mui pe,* which
means, "just the wisdom of a young coconut tree." It is a humble
reminder, in advance, that if I make a mistake, I should remember
that I am only a young coconut in the plantation.

Rock and sand are two important natural resources in Oceania. (I
am using the word *Oceania* in this article, instead of *Pacific.*) Pacific
is a word that was imposed by the colonial empire on the people of
Oceania, without consultation. It is a word that portrays the smallness
of the island nations in the Pacific Ocean. On one hand, the term
Pacific is derogatory and signifies powerlessness. *Oceania* on the
other hand depicts the notion of wholeness and equality.

Oceania is actually the combination of the land space and the ocean.
Land + ocean + underground = Oceania. Therefore, Oceania is not
small as it has been claimed. Oceania is big and vast when compared
to any of the world's continents.[6]

Most of the island nations in Oceania have these two resources, sand
and rock, in their make up. Aotearoa New Zealand is part of Oceania
and possesses rich natural resources of rock and sand. My family and
I live at St. Clair, which is very close to the beach. Quite often I take

---

6.   c.f. 'Epeli Hau'ofa, *"Sea of Islands,"* in Inside Out, 24-52

a walk to the beach and enjoy watching the beauty of nature. At the beach I have been astounded by the elegance of sand and rocks. The sound of the wind and the coming of sea breezes create an atmosphere that is natural and harmonious. In addition, the splendour of the open sea and its big waves rolling in from the deep towards the land, create a wonderfully diverse melody of sounds.

As the waves roll toward the land some of them arrive on the sandy beach and produce quiet and peaceful sounds of harmony. Other waves arrive on the rocks, and produce a roaring sound and a commotion that is uncontrollable. As I watch these lively experiences of nature, I am reminded about human relationships and their complexity. Some are quite friendly and others are quite hostile. Then I ask some critical questions which lead me into some further questions. How can we deal constructively with confrontational issues? Can we live in harmony in the midst of our diversity? What is the appropriate way of dealing with our differences? These questions might not lead us to a final answer, but they can encourage further conversations on how to be more tolerant in our relationships with others who have different points of views to ours. In order to lead us to a possible solution I see sand as a metaphor or symbol for building good relationships, in contrast to rock.

The Bible portrays a negative image of sand as inferior to rock. Jesus specifically told his disciples the story of the two builders (Matthew 7:24-25). The wise builder built his house on the rock as it is more stable and also able to confront the cruelty of nature, but the foolish builder built his house on the sand, which symbolises weakness and powerlessness. Some of the Psalms speak of rock as a metaphor for the mighty hands of God. For example Psalm 18:2,

> "The Lord is my rock, my fortress and my deliverer,
> my God, my rock in whom I take refuge."

In the Middle East, rocks can become shelters in a sand storm and fortresses for when enemies attack. Using rock as a metaphor for God is pertinent in their context, but for us in Oceania, it is the antithesis, especially after the recent Christchurch earthquakes. It opens our eyes to know that rocks do not always protect houses, but can also destroy houses and threaten lives.

Therefore, sand from an Oceanic perspective symbolises flexibility, openness, tolerance, and acceptance. The dictionary defines *sand* as small loose grains of worn or disintegrated rock. Although this definition still links sand to rock, it is in a different fashion. The nature of sand is losing and opening. These grains are not lying individually but collectively with open spaces. Their strength comes from their connectedness and their openness. When the big waves roll down onto the grains of sand, they sink quietly because they can find spaces to enter and fill up, but when they reach the rock they produce violent noises and cruel confrontations.

I believe that if Jesus was growing up in Oceania he would use 'sand' in one of his parables as a metaphor for God's unconditional love and acceptance, rather than rock. Rock can't stop the rolling of the waves but the grains of sand can, because they have spaces to go gently in between. To build strong relationships we must work collectively and allow spaces for others to function in and to grow. The Season of Pentecost reminds us as well of the success of the early followers of Jesus, because of their collective efforts and their openness for others to share in the power of God's Spirit. Rock can't, but sand can.

Sand Can but Snow Can't

An Oceanic metaphor for forgiveness:
the Christian response when life gets tough.

My previous article in *Connections* was titled, "Rock Can't but Sand Can." In that article I made a comparison between rock and sand as a real life experience in nature and how it became a metaphor for any kind of human relationship. In this article, I compare sand and snow, and hopefully we can extract from it another metaphor for good, Christian living. Sand and snow are both components of the natural environment, but they do not stay together or mix well with each other. However, their commonality and differences make them special in their contribution to our natural world. They both contribute to the beauty of nature.

Since our arrival in Dunedin at the beginning of this year we have admired the beauty of St. Clair's sandy beach close to where we live. On a sunny day we can stand at one end of the beach and look to the other end with admiration for its beauty, purity and whiteness. It is so clean that it reflects the sun's rays into our eyes, so we need to wear sunglasses. However, my experience of the cleanness of the sandy beach was changed by my first experience of snow on Sunday 24 July 2011.

As a person who came from the tropical island of Tonga, my first experience of real snow brought a mixture of surprise and excitement. I was surprised that the whiteness and the beauty of the snow covered the purity of the sand. It was also an exciting experience for my family and I as our first experience of real snow! In our excitement we drove from one place to the other to view the beauty of the snow, despite the danger of slippery roads. It was indeed the whiteness and the purity of the snow that attracted our attention. No wonder Psalm 51:7 uses 'snow' to symbolise the abundance of God's forgiveness. In that verse the Psalm says,

"Purge me with hyssop, and I shall be clean; wash me, and I shall be whiter than snow."

The Psalmist doesn't use sand, as it is not pure enough to compare with the power of God's forgiveness. Instead he uses snow as a more appropriate metaphor.

However, looking at it from an Oceanic perspective, snow is not able to endure the harshness of Oceania's weather. Most of the island nations in Oceania have a tropical climate. They don't have snow, but they have white sandy beaches. Since we have been in New Zealand, we have spent most of our time in Auckland. While we were in Auckland we never experienced snow, but we always went swimming in the sea, alongside white sandy beaches. We were always thrilled by the purity of the sand and its coolness during Summer time.

We also admired the capacity of the sand to withstand the power of big waves and stormy weather. Sand will never give up or back off. It will always endure and persevere even when the season is changing. Snow on the other hand, cannot survive the changing of the weather. Summer weather will cause the snow to melt! The purity and whiteness of snow can be seen only when the weather remains cold, but when circumstances change, the snow melts. Although snow and sand are both important parts of the natural world, only sand can maintain its beauty and purity when things heat up and the journey gets tough.

As I continue to look with anticipation at the contrasting performances of sand and snow, they bring to mind how we behave and our attitudes when life gets tough. How do we react when we are in difficult circumstances? What does our Christian faith teach us about times when life is hard to bear? Can we still maintain our human integrity when circumstances are changing?

It is tempting to give up when things are not going well. If there is a time for facing tough situations, it is the present time. We look around the world and its current affairs and we worry. Increased violence in many parts of the world, the loss of jobs and the lack of employment worry many low income families. Crime among young people is increasing, and the increase in poverty is a major concern among our communities.

In the church, we are concerned about declining membership, the increasing cost of ministry, the need to provide a ministry that is effective for our youth, and also the overusing of the same people in various responsibilities in the church. Surely, the easiest thing to do at these times is to escape and run away. If we were to do this however, we would lose our integrity and identity as God's people. As followers of Christ, let us never forget that we have "sandy ingredients" to uphold. Sand can but snow can't. Snow is whiter and purer, but sand can be tougher in hard times – and still maintain its purity.

I believe that if the writer of Psalm 51 had grown up in Oceania he would have used sand instead of snow as a metaphor for God's enduring forgiveness, as emphasised in verse 7. The Psalm therefore would be rewritten,

> "Purge me with hyssop, and I shall be clean; wash me, and I shall be whiter than sand."

Sand can be used as a metaphor for both purity and endurance. So when you next visit the beach and see sand, or think about sand, let sand remind you about our Christian tradition of perseverance in hard times as a vital part of our call to discipleship. Dietrich Bonhoeffer in his book *The Cost of Discipleship*, claims that the call to follow Christ is a call to endure suffering moments. Sand can but snow can't. Enjoy your next visit to the beach.

Kuo Fonua e Hakau: The Reef is Land

*A Tongan Concept of Justice toward Children in Relation
to the Words of Jesus in Luke 18:17.*

Tenā koutou tenā tātou katoa, Ta lofa lava, Bula vinaka, Malo e lelei,
and warm Pacific greetings. The topic of my presentation is *Kuo
Fonua e Hakau,* meaning, 'The Reef is Land.' *Hakau* (reef) on one
hand could metaphorically refer to youthfulness like the early stage
of the process to become a land space. *Fonua* on the other hand refers
to an inhabited place or land space where the inhabitants live and
cultivate.

This Tongan word *fonua* has a parallel connotation among some of the
Oceania languages. For instance, in Maori the word for *fonua* (land)
is *whenua* (land, placenta), in Fijian is *vanua* (land), and in Samoan
is *fanua* (land, placenta). Their meanings are closely related and they
seem to refer to an inhabited place or space. Using this concept – *Kuo
fonua e hakau* – depicts the uniqueness of *hakau* (reef) as a living and
an inhabited place or space.

The reef is both a living and an inhabited place for hundreds of sea
creatures. A reef is also at the same time an inhabited place for the
livelihood of hundreds of the inhabitants of Oceania. It means that
fonua does not necessarily refer to dry land only, but it also refers to
any place that could provide shelter, security and nourishment.

Fonua has four meanings in Tongan. Firstly, it refers to the mother's
womb where a baby is developed, protected, sheltered and nourished.
Secondly, it refers to the landscape where people can live, be protected,
and be nourished. Thirdly, it refers to the grave where the dead are
sheltered, protected and nourished. Fourthly, it refers to people that
inhabit the land. We have a Tongan saying, "*Fonua pe tangata,*"
meaning "land is people." These understandings of land (*fonua*)
identify *fonua* as a place of protection, shelter and nourishment.
Therefore, using this concept, *Kuo fonua e hakau* emphasises the

importance and uniqueness of reef as a metaphor for children as the *fonua*, "*Fonua pe tangata.*"

If people are part of the land, then children, who are part of the people, are a vital part of the structure. In this presentation, I would like to use this concept to identify and explore the uniqueness and value of children, as opposed to the way they are often perceived and treated in our society and the world.

We shouldn't wait to value our children in the light of their future potential, in the same way we think about the reef and its natural processes, but rather we should value them, now for they are the *fonua* (land) now. This concept might seem contrary to the traditional Tongan concept of *Hakau e lolotonga ko e fonua e kaha'u*, meaning, 'The reef of today is the land of the future.' This traditional concept seems to make an assumption that the reef can only be important and valued when it becomes an inhabited land or an island. The concept that I will develop in this presentation is to value children as *fonua* (land) now, rather than at sometime in the future.

There are four components that I would like to emphasise about the significance of children. They highlight some of the injustices that they face. Firstly, children as *fonua* are not worthless. Secondly, children as *fonua* are vulnerable. Thirdly, children as *fonua* are connected beings. Finally, I will use the words of Jesus in Luke 18:16-17 to verify my position in fighting against the injustices that are imposed upon children. I have to admit that I am not an expert in the areas of childhood education or the social issues that our children face, like child poverty and child abuse. However, the intention of my presentation is to trigger conversations and also to raise awareness of the reality of the injustices that children confront in our society.

Children as *Fonua* are Not Worthless

Children are not worthless, our future depends on them. Giving our children the resources they need to be nourished and grow, builds up families, communities and nations. They need support and understanding in the early stage of their journey in order for those resources to be protected and produced. I asked my wife, who is a pre-school teacher, about her view of children. She responded that children do have the material resources they need to progress and develop, but they also need to be cherished and nourished in order to flourish and be productive. The word *nourish* means to "build up, strengthen, develop and sharpen" and *cherish* means to "treasure, value, protect and celebrate."

In the curriculum book used by pre-schools and their staff to guide their daily operation, titled *Te Whariki*, it states,

> "Each child learns in his or her own way. The curriculum builds on a child's current needs, strengths and interests by allowing children choices and by encouraging them to take responsibility for their own learning." (*Te Whariki*, p. 20)

From this statement we affirm that, children are all capable of learning. Children are not lacking in mental, physical and spiritual resources but they do need support, understanding and guidance. Furthermore, children need to be valued and upheld as they develop their personal and cultural identities.

For us who are parents, we notice that whenever we ignore our children's excitement to show us their achievements they immediately feel let down and even pessimistic about themselves. In addition, they feel that we are not interested in them. Furthermore, they think that their achievement is not good enough to be acknowledged and celebrated. Such adult reactions are absolutely discouraging and disempowering for children. Children deserve to be recognised. However, in many circumstances their achievements are ignored and even undermined.

This is the case in many situations. Children are viewed as ignorant, with limited minds. They are often invisible in many conversations and in the decision making process, because they are regarded as unwise and inexperienced. For instance, when adults are talking and suddenly a child joins in. That child would be told off for interrupting them, (in Tongan "*Kaui-talanoa*"). That child is seen as an unnecessary interruption because he/she is not wise or experienced enough to be part of the conversation. In many cultural contexts, children are viewed as silly, dumb-headed, crazy, lazy and cunning. These negative attitudes are man-made, and aim to confine children to an inferior place in the family social structure. This kind of attitude will disempower children.

Helen Morton in her book entitled, *Becoming Tongan*, claims that the misbehaviour of children in their social life, is to do with the put down words that they hear from their parents and adult members of the community. Morton states,

> "These are negatively valued characteristics, the most commonly mentioned being that children are *vale* and *pau'u* (naughty, mischievous)." (Morton, p. 72)

Children deserve to be treated with love and understanding. They need to be cherished in order to flourish, which in turn will build their confidence and aid their human development. When people are respected, they will not only feel worthy, but they will also feel confident in what they do. Children should expect their society to respect them. They want to be seen as being as acceptable as other age groups in their community.

The resources that support children come from their surroundings, like families, the community (*kāinga*), church and nation. Furthermore, those resources will shape their identity and their values. The traditional understanding of home as the first institution for children's learning indicates the importance of parenting. Parents are the first teachers to equip and cherish children's mental, physical and spiritual development. Kent and Barbara Hughes in the book entitled, *Common Sense Parenting*, remark,

> "Parents, like archers, launch their children into the future, aiming toward a distant target. Some parents take clear aim, and their arrows are well directed toward their future mark. But other children's arrows are fired from unsteady bows, parents who are, at best, ambivalent about where they came from and unsure of their aim. Their arrows waver and falter, then finally succumb to gravity with no mark in sight. They tragically prove the adage, 'If you aim at nothing, you'll surely hit it.'" (Hughes, p. 4)

It is the role of parents together with the wider kinship group (*kāinga/ ainga*) to ensure that children are protected, supported, and cherished in order to flourish.

Children as *Fonua* are Vulnerable

It may be true that children are resourceful, but they are at the same time vulnerable members of the society. They are vulnerable in the same way as the reef. I mentioned in my abstract, the nature of the vulnerability that the reef encountered when France held their nuclear tests at Mururoa atoll in Tahiti between 1966 and 1996. The coral reef died, together with the sea creatures that depended on the reef for security, shelter and sustenance. Recently, marine scientists discovered that parts of the Great Barrier Reef in Australia are dying due to global warming and climate change. I am sure the treatment of the Pacific Ocean by powerful nations as a rubbish dump for their toxic waste will have a detrimental impact on most of the coral reefs of Oceania. Reefs are vulnerable just as children are, and they suffered a great deal because of negligence and exploitation. Children are vulnerable because they are weak, powerless and defenceless.

Children are victims of sexual and physical abuse because they are powerless to defend themselves. It is a horrible experience to see that many children are suffering abuse in their own homes and under the care of their parents and care-givers. Right to Life New Zealand in their 2016 report declared that,

> "New Zealand, which has a population a 4.47 million, has one of the highest rates of child abuse in the developed world. It also has one of the worst rates of child death by maltreatment within the family. NZ Police respond to one 'family violence' call every seven minutes. Police say that in 60% of domestic violence cases, children are also being abused..."[7]

The media has reported major cases about the horror of child abuse. We remember today those children who suffered appalling abuse before they were killed. These children were Lily Bing, Nia Glassie,

---

7. 'Child Abuse – When will NZ Recognise that it Commences in the Womb?' Ken Orr. Accessed from: https://righttolife.org.nz/2016/05/31/child-abuse-when-will-nz-recognise-that-it-commences-in-the-womb/#more-6595

Mikara Riti and the three months old twins, Chris and Cru Kahui, and most recently there was the cruel death of Moko Rangitoheriri, just to name a few. Right to Life New Zealand reported that, "Every year twelve children die from appalling physical and sexual abuse."[8] Their names are engraved on our minds. May we never forget these beautiful children and the shame of their death.

Children are victims of exploitation as well as of violence when they are still in their mother's womb. If the mother's womb is *fonua*, a place of security, shelter and nourishment, then why have so many lives been exploited and violated in the womb. I have to admit that I am neither a medical professional nor a person with the experience of a mid-wife, but I am a professional carer who cares for the life of every human being. One of my roles as a minister, is to provide pastoral care to all age groups in my community, including pregnant mothers. They have to be cared for and protected, together with the babies in their wombs. This is not the case in many situations in our nation.

Right to Life New Zealand also reported,

> "While 61 born children have died as a result of non-accidental injuries in New Zealand in the last 10 years, 153,819 children have been killed in the womb as a result of deliberate injuries inflicted by a doctor (2005 to 2014). To put this in to perspective, there are over 2500 unborn children killed by violence, for every born child killed by violence."[9]

I believe all of us have duty to protect these innocent lives and it is appalling to see the violation and exploitation of babies in the *fonua* (wombs) of their mothers. What shall we do as a community to protect these innocent lives?

Children are victims of economic marginalization. They are marginalized because they are powerless and perceived as ignorant. In many poor communities, like our Pacific communities, our children are victims of economic marginalization because of the inequality that our families face in this nation.

---

8. Ibid
9. Ibid

In a book entitled, *Inequality – A New Zealand Crisis* edited by Max Rashbrooke, he states,

> "When people have hugely different incomes, they have different opportunities – and these differences can persist through generations." (*Inequality*, p. 9)

This statement is real for many Pacific families. According to many surveys and reports, many of our Pacific families live under the poverty line. They live under the poverty line because of the inequality of incomes that they have. These differences definitely have a huge impact on child poverty. Child poverty is a serious and prolonged social problem that we face in this country. Children are economically deprived in their homes and families.

According to a 2012 report from Dr Russell Wills, the Children's Commissioner, in New Zealand, "…as many as 25 percent of children currently live in poverty. This is about 270,000 children."[10]

It is estimated that spending only an extra 3% of the government's annual budget or around 6 billion dollars would solve the problem of child poverty in this nation. These figures are estimates but they show the extent of child poverty among our families. Children are going to school without lunches and without decent clothes to keep them warm in winter. Children have diseases that are cause by poor housing conditions where they live. Sicknesses like asthma, eczema, colds, and flu are common health issues among children who live under the poverty line. If children continue to face these conditions, then we can expect unhealthy children in our society. Poverty is a huge obstacle to our children's whole human development. Can we solve this problem? How can we address the issue of child poverty?

I believe there is no one single answer to the issue of poverty because it has multiple causes. However, one solution might be to close the gap between the haves and the have nots, the poor and the rich. If poverty is caused by inequality, as Max Rasbrooke claimed, then we have to break that barrier.

---

10. 'Solutions to Child Poverty in New Zealand: Evidence for Action.' Accessed from: https://www.occ.org.nz/assets/Uploads/EAG/Final-report/Final-report-Solutions-to-child-poverty-evidence-for-action.pdf

Richard Wilkinson and Kate Pickett in their book entitled, *The Spirit Level*, state,

> "The evidence shows that reducing inequality is the best way of improving the equality of the social environment, and so the real quality of life, for all of us." (Wilkin and Pickett, p. 29)

Nelson Mandela also remarks,

> "Poverty is not natural. It is man-made and it can be overcome and eradicated by the actions of human beings."[11]

Wilkin and Picket's, and Mandela's ideals can be achieved if those who hold the power, namely the government, have the will to break down financial barriers. After the government announced their budget for the new Financial Year, I asked the Director of the Methodist Mission Southern, Ms Laura Black, whether this budget deals with the problem of child poverty. Her answer was a clear "No." The big winners of this budget are the middle class families. This means that the problem of child poverty will continue to exist in our society because thousands of families are still under the poverty line.

Children as *Fonua* are Connected

Because children are living beings and members of families and communities, they are living in connection. They are connected like reefs with their natural surroundings and their survival depends on that connection. When that connection is jeopardised or damaged, children's lives are at risk. For instance, children who are growing up in broken families are likely to be at risk in society. Bruce Logan in his book entitled, *Waking Up to Marriage*, states, that,

> "One in five children under the age of 12 months live in fatherless households." (Logan, p. 37)

Many of these children no longer have a connection with both of their parents, who are expected to be their first teachers in their first institution, which is the home. (Logan, p. 39) Losing connection with their parents can mean that they will also lose the instruction and

---

11. Accessed from: https://www.cpag.org.nz/assets/Welfare%20Reform/101101%20 What%20We%20Heard%20WWG.pdf

advice that children need to guide them in positive social interactions with others. Furthermore, they may start to listen to the wrong people and the wrong advice, which may lead them into trouble. Logan continues,

> "Of juveniles and young adults serving in long-term correction facilities, 70 percent did not live with both parents while growing up." (Logan, p. 37)

Children who are disconnected from their parents and families are more likely to end up in the wrong places with the wrong people. These children are more likely to be victims of exploitation and oppression by opportunists. These children are easily lured by these criminals without their consent because they lose the connection with parents and families. In many cultural contexts, children are forced into the sex industry and slave labour. Save the Children New Zealand reported that children who are disconnected from their families and communities are easy targets for these criminal organizations. Their disconnection from their natural surroundings – families and communities – distances them from their security, shelter and sustenance.

Just as *Fonua* cannot survive without connection with their natural surroundings, so it is with children. Children are a vital part of the strands which families and society are weaving together. If the strand of children is disconnected, the whole of the family and the social structures will collapse. Like a mat that gains its strength from weaving together all the strands, so it is with families and society. Children must have a space in the whole pattern in order for families and society to stand strong. How can we ensure that this connection is maintained? Who is responsible for upholding this connection? Let me reflect on Jesus' attitude toward children as a paradigm for building connection with children.

Jesus' Attitude toward Children in Luke 18:16-17

Before I comment about Jesus' attitude toward children in the gospel of Luke, I would like to put this passage into context. The story of Jesus' welcoming of children, according to Luke's account, comes after two short stories. The first story is about a widow who was seeking justice and is an example of the affect of persistent prayer (Luke 18:1-8). Her search for justice was finally granted. This story concludes with the words of Jesus. He says,

> "And will not God grant justice to his chosen ones who cry
> to him day and night? Will he delay long in helping them?
> I tell you, he will quickly grant justice to them."

The second story is about a Pharisee and a tax-collector who went to the temple to pray (Luke 18:9-14.) In their prayers, they both beseeched God for justice. Of course they had their own ways of expressing their longing for justice. This story concludes with the words of Jesus. He says,

> "I tell you, this man (tax-collector) went down to his home
> justified rather than the other (Pharisee)."

These two early stories in chapter 18 highlight the significance of justice as a vital part of Jesus' ministry. These stories prepare us for the third story in chapter 18, about parents who brought their children to Jesus to be blessed and healed. These children were rejected by his disciples, but Jesus intervened and welcomed them.

This story in Luke has parallel references in Matthew 19:13-15 and Mark 10:13-16. Although the synoptic gospels all told this story in a similar way, Luke bases his version of the story closely on the gospel of Mark. The way both Mark and Luke structure this story is similar. This story starts with parents who brought their children to Jesus to be blessed. His disciples rejected them and chased them away. When Jesus saw the attitude of his disciples he was disappointed and intervened to welcome these children. He said,

> "Let the little children come to me, and do not stop them;
> for it is such as these that the kingdom of God belongs.
> Truly I tell you, whoever does not receive the kingdom of
> God as a little child will never enter it."

There are three important aspects of Jesus' actions that show his positive attitude toward children. The first aspect is his open-armed acceptance of children (Come to me and do not stop them). The second aspect is his rebuking of his disciples for rejecting these little children (Do not stop them). The third aspect is his linking of the kingdom of God to children (It is to such as these that the kingdom of God belongs).

The word 'kingdom' derives from a Greek word, '*basileia*,' which means 'kingdom, reign and rule.' When the synoptic gospels talk about the 'kingdom of God,' they refer to the 'reign and rule of God.' The kingdom of God is not a domain or estate but is about the rule and reign of God, taking place in someone's life. When Jesus uses the word 'kingdom' in this context, he links entry into the rule and the reign of God to the simplicity and openness of children. Entry into the kingdom is something that we receive freely without any human effort for it is God's gift. If God's kingdom is a gift, then children can also share in it alongside other members of the community. Justo Gonzalez in his commentary on Luke's gospel states,

> "The kingdom belongs to them, and to us, out of God's sheer, unmerited favour." (*Luke*, p. 214)

The actions of Jesus reflect his attitude toward children, which is contrary to the attitude of his disciples, who represent the common perception of his society toward children. Gonzalez comments on these kinds of attitudes during Jesus' time.

> "In the Greco-Roman world, it was perfectly legal to abandon a child you did not wish to raise. Children were commonly seen as a source of family income in the future, and of security in old age – or as a way to pass on the family name and traditions." (p. 214)

While the disciples represent the attitude of adults towards children, Jesus acted in a different manner. He welcomed, valued and included children as unique members of his community and also the kingdom of God. Children may be different in terms of age and responsibilities, but in the eyes of God they are the same as everyone else. Jesus' action embodies the God of justice who seeks to defend the weak.

Conclusion

In conclusion, I would like to say that the way children are treated and perceived today is no different from two thousand years ago. Children suffer because they are weak, powerless and defenceless. Many are victims of abuse, exploitation and cruelty in their families, communities and society. Children are longing and crying for justice and if our society continues to turn deaf ears to their plight, more children will die.

Holomui Kimu'a: Reversing To The Front

A Tongan Concept of Building Church in the 21ˢᵗ Century.

Introduction

It is appropriate to both look back and move forward as we determine how to maintain the existence of our church in the 21ˢᵗ century. In looking back we learn from the weaknesses and the strengths of the past that could help to shape a vibrant future. If there was no past, there is no present and no future. The Tongan notion of *holomui kimu'a* denotes the understanding of reversing to the front. *Holomui* means "reverse" and *kimu'a* means, to the "front."

This concept derives from the way Tongans row their canoes. They look backward and row their canoes forward. By looking backward they can use their full strength to row the canoe and at the same time concentrate on rowing, rather than on the distance left to travel. Looking backward captures in our imagination the importance of the past. If we only focus on the future we don't know where we came from and might easily give up before we arrive at our destination. In order for the church to improve and strengthen its ministry, it has to look back to its past and anticipate the journey ahead with a clear vision of the future.

The word 'church' derives from a Greek word, *ekkelesia* (ecclesia), which means 'assembly, gathering or church.' This definition clearly indicates that the church is not a building or an institution, but the people. Without people there is no church and there is no building for people to gather in. The first appearance of this word *ekkelesia* in the scriptures is in Matthew 16, verse 18 when Jesus responded to Peter's confession that 'he is the Messiah, the Son of the living God.' In his response, Jesus says,

> "And I tell you, you are Peter, and on this rock I will build my *church* (ekkelesia), and the gates of Hades will not prevail against it."

The word 'church' appears 114 times in the New Testament and it's understood differently in different contexts according to the writer's individual opinion. It is used for local communities, as well as in a universal sense, to mean all believers.

As the gospel was proclaimed and Christianity spread all over the world, the understanding of *church* changed. It was started in the Jewish community, for the first followers of Jesus were all Jews. Their understanding of their identity as the covenant people of God influenced their view of the church. People from other ethnic groups became proselytes before they joined the church. The church started as a movement within the Jewish religion and everyone who decided to join this movement had to first become a Jew. However, through the ministry of Paul, the gospel was proclaimed to non-Jews and the understanding of church changed. Everyone is included, for God's love is for all people. This is what Paul called *grace* (*charis*). which refers to God's gift of universal love. Both Jews and Gentiles had equal access to the church through faith. Over time, the church separated itself from Judaism. It developed its own theology that enhances everyone's faith and participation in ministry.

Christianity was not only established in Middle Eastern countries, but spread to Europe through the work of missionaries. Their efforts of proclaiming the gospel spread it beyond the Mediterranean basin to other parts of the world. Missionaries eventually reached the uttermost parts of the world, proclaiming the good news of Jesus Christ. People who believed in their message were baptised and joined the church (*ekkelesia*). The church spread into different geographical locations and cultural contexts that shaped the understanding of church. The development of different theologies, church structures and church polity were influenced by these diverse contexts. Their cultural, theological, ecclesiological and hermeneutical methodologies influenced a great deal of our understanding of church.

These various contextual approaches created by past generations are still full of meaning for the current generation in the church. Today, we turn around and look back to our past, with a vision of a future that has hope. We look back and wonder what we can do differently to promote the mission of God in the life of the church in the 21ˢᵗ century, and especially in our Dunedin Methodist Parish.

- Is our practice of ministry still relevant today?

- Are our doctrines and church structure able to enrich our faith today?

- Do we have methods of outreach that attract people to our church?

- How can we grow our church in the 21ˢᵗ century?

In order for our church to preserve its future, it has to look back and learn from its past failures and successes. There are two important components of *holomui kimu'a* (reversing to the front). Firstly, its capacity to learn from history, and secondly its capacity to form a vision for the future.

History

History is about the events of the past and all the components attached to them. *Holomui kimu'a* stresses the importance of looking backward to our history in order to move forward. We can't change or develop a new vision without looking to our past. Looking to our past will give us clear direction toward our future.

As Methodists we are a people with a history. We are descendants of our forebears in the Methodist family, who had sets of values, doctrines and theologies that developed out of their contexts. Methodism from the outset was a movement and it has a tendency to move constantly. John Wesley, the founder of Methodism, believed strongly that the church was established to look outward rather than look inward. He developed a theology that God's salvation is for all people. God's love is not confined to any particular elite group of people, but is for the whole world. This kind of theology influenced his understanding of church. He saw the church as not being fenced in, but open to everyone. His well-known words sum it all up when he says, "The world is my parish."

Our history reminds us that we are a movement and our mission should not be limited within the four walls of our church. As a parish we need to widen our vision, as John Wesley widened his vision about the mission of the church. This means we need to continue to explore different ways of becoming an effective church in the 21st century.

One of the strengths of the Methodist Movement in its early stages was the Class Meeting. This was unique to the growth of Methodism. The idea of the Class Meeting is to build strong bond among the local church members and also enable spiritual nourishment. I remember when I grew up in the Methodist Church in Tonga, the impact that the Class Meeting had in my life and my faith. This is a practice that is still strong in the Tongan congregations in the islands as well as overseas, especially the Methodist Tongans. Some English speaking churches are adopting John's Wesley concept of 'Class Meetings' but they rename them as 'Cell Groups.' The name might be different, but the principles and ideas of forming these groups, are the same.

Evangelism was another strength of the Methodist Movement. John Wesley believed that the proclamation of the gospel should not be confined within the four walls of the church. Wesley was an ordained Anglican minister, who was barred from preaching in Anglican churches. Common people were also not welcome in churches, which is why Wesley decided to proclaim the gospel by preaching in the open air and open spaces like mines, streets and highways. He proclaimed a gospel of inclusiveness, and believed that all people can be saved by God's grace.

The question that we wrestle with today is, 'What kind of evangelism is effective in the 21st century?' One aspect of outreach in the early part of the Methodist Movement was charitable work and prison visits. John Wesley and the early Methodists were passionate about providing support and hospitality to the poor people in their society. They were keen to make a positive transformation in people's lives. These early Methodists were trying their best to be a church that could practise what they preached. They tried to maintain the values that John Wesley claimed, "Do all the good you can…"

Vision for the future

The *Holomui kimu'a* concept anticipates full participation and endurance during the course of voyage. The rowers are rowing with their backs to the front, but with a vision to reach to their destination. While they are rowing backwards they turn their backs to the challenges of the current, waves and the wind, and focus on the task that they are engaging in. At the same time they envision a destination that will be full of new surprises, which will determine their future hope. This hope will certainly demand a change in our way of thinking and doing things. We cannot be the same as we were when we started our journey. We can look back and learn from our past, but without being ready to change there will no vision and certainly no hope.

Synods, parishes and congregations across the connexion have met many times to discuss the future of our church and we have come up with good ideas that we need to consider as part of our strategies and visions for the growth of our church. Here are some thoughts:

- We shall seek to establish the nourishment of the spirit.

- Work in partnership with the Spirit of God.

- Understanding Jesus and his ministry to world today.

- Addressing diversity, openness and inclusiveness.

- Seeking a sustainable model of church that will continue into the future.

Strategies:

- Passionate Worship

- Outreach for wholeness

- Pastoral Care and Radical Hospitality

- Equipping and Sending

- Inspiring Music

The past is history, today is a reality, and the future is a dream. Our dream will come true if we act together to create and implement a strategy that works for our church today.

Fonua pe Tangata: A Tongan Migrant Perspective in Relation to the Words of Matthew 4:15

Introduction

Ni Sa Bula Vinaka, Talalofa Lava, Kia Ora, Malo e lelei, and warm Pasifika greetings. I am glad that some of the things that I planned to talk about have been mentioned and discussed by our previous presenters. I hope that I won't repeat what others have already said, especially about the connection of people and land in a metaphorical way. However, I am aware that the theme that I propose here is unique in its own right, because the emphasis is not so much on people who are settling on their land in Tonga, but rather on those in the diaspora. In this case, to be more specific it refers to Tongans who live overseas, but still feel strongly connected to their land in Tonga. These people either have families still living in Tonga, business commitments in Tonga or an ancestral piece of land that they could return to and cultivate in the future. They see themselves as the extension of their families and land, as they move to other parts of the world, searching for opportunities in the diaspora that will benefit them and those back home. Their strong connection to their land in Tonga denotes the Tongan concept of *Fonua pe tangata*, which means, "land is people."

This presentation aims to convey the viewpoint that although people have departed from their homeland, they are still connected with it, for that's where they were born and raised, and their umbilical cord was cut and buried. This viewpoint promotes the importance of belonging and ownership and asks these important questions:

- What is land?

- Where is our land boundary?

- Who owns the land?

These questions alert us to the importance of land ownership, identity and cultural, customary and family boundaries.

- Do those who left the island nations have any right to their land?

- Do they feel connected to their land of birth?

I ask these questions because I will try to answer them in this presentation, and at the same time pose a challenge to those who live in our island nation, especially the government in Tonga that assumes that once someone has left their ancestral land in Tonga, he/she shouldn't have any legal right to it.

The *Fonua pe tangata* concept signifies the importance of people and their connection with the land. The way people cultivate and utilize their piece of land in Tonga for the benefit of their families, is related to the way Tongans labour and toil in industries overseas for similar purposes. This special bond between people and land in this Tongan concept emphasises the link between people and land in Matthew 4:15,

> "Land of Zebulun and land of Naphtali along the sea, beyond the Jordan River. This is Galilee where the non-Jewish people live."

Matthew quoted these words from Isaiah 9:1-2, which are part of Isaiah's prophecy of the dawn of a new day, when God's agent, a liberator, would intervene to set God's people free from those who would come to grab their land, namely the Assyrians. It is a messianic prophecy, which shows God's concern for the land and the land owners. God's act of love and kindness would not separate the people from the land. When the people are liberated, their lands are also liberated. As Isaiah prophesied,

> "But suddenly there will be no more gloom for the land that suffered. In the past God made the lands of Zebulun and Naphtali hang their heads in shame, but in the future those lands will be made great. They will stretch from the road along the Mediterranean Sea to the land beyond the Jordan River and north to Galilee, the land of people who are not Israelites."

These words from Isaiah and from Matthew emphasise the importance of *fonua pe tangata*, land is people. They are inseparable.

Scope of *Fonua pe Tangata* Concept

If land and people can't be separated, then it is right to claim that people without their land are a lost people. This is true for those who are forced from their land because of natural disaster, war, violence, persecution or oppression. They are separated from their land against their will and therefore they are people with no clear future. Yet, they will always remember and long to return to their land because that is a vital part of their identity. To lose their land is to lose part of their life. Therefore, the *fonua pe tangata* concept makes a claim that it is an injustice to separate people (*tangata*) from their land (*fonua*) for the following reasons.

Firstly, *fonua pe tangata* values people. It doesn't mean that land is less valuable, but conveys a point of view that the benefits and value of land are shown when the inhabitants cultivate and utilize the land for the welfare of their communities. When there are no people to cultivate the land or even to share the obligations that go with the land (*tauhi fonua*, meaning, "caretaker of land"), then as in funerals and weddings, we can hear a voice, saying, *me'a ongo ko e masiva tangata/ fefine*, meaning, "It is with pity that we see the shortage/poverty of people." Poverty of people can lead to the poverty of land, which can lead to communal poverty. When land is not cultivated because there are no people or there is a shortage of people, then it can become a waste land, especially where shortage of land is an issue. In special circumstances, landowners who live overseas can initiate agreements with those who live in Tonga to continue cultivating their lands for the benefit of their community.

Secondly, *fonua pe tangata* values ancestral connection. Every family has their ancestral land and they find their meaning and value in their attachment to it (Jione Havea, "Reading Islandly," *Voices from the Margin*, p. 83; Iutisone Salevao; Ilaitia Tuwere). They may leave and go to other countries, but their connection to their ancestors remains in their connection with their ancestral land. To take away their land will not only alienate them from their ancestors but also their roots. Their land belongs to their ancestors, and holds their histories and stories. To lose their land is to lose their stories and histories and therefore lose their connection with their ancestors.

Jione Havea remarks,

> "The whenua/land represents that which makes one indigenous to a location; whenua/land is not property to be sold or owned but a home that makes one feel s/he belongs." (*Voices From The Margin*, p. 83).

Thirdly, *fonua pe tangata* exhibits flexibility and mobility in the relationship of people and land. People are always on the verge of moving for different reasons and purposes. But as they move, they maintain their strong bond to their land through remittances, family reunions, acts of charity, important church occasions and through family celebrations like funerals, weddings and birthdays. Their commitments to such responsibilities demonstrate their allegiance to their ancestral land and *kāinga* in the island. They see themselves as an extension of their land in the island, for their sustenance and wellbeing. 'Inoke Hu'akau, a Tongan migrant in Australia, alluded to this view in an article.

> "But I will also remind our Legislative Assembly that Tonga as a nation cannot survive economically without the Tongan diaspora overseas. Our King has asked us regardless of where you are to work together and rebuild Tonga." ("Illegal-activity vs time", *Matangitonga*, 22 March 2018)

I don't know whether this is true for every Tongan in the diaspora, but it is certainly true for many Tongans who still have compassion for the affairs of those back in the island nation.

Fourthly, *fonua pe tangata* values a place to live. It means we can't separate people from land. They are inseparable because land provides a home and a place of sustenance. To separate or to take away that place would impose homelessness and displacement upon individuals and people. This is what happens to refugees and asylum-seekers who are forced to leave their homes because of violence. They search around the world for a place that they can call home. People require a land to live in and cultivate to feel at home, to identify with and to experience real freedom.

Some land grabbers and exploiters treat vacant land in the islands as an opportunity to claim or seize land. This is what happened in one of the cases that came out in *Matangitonga* newspaper on 22 March 2018. The title of the article was 'Illegal-activity vs time.' The writer of this article ('Inoke Fotu Hu'akau) asks these questions.

> "Are we saying that an illegal activity of an illegal land grab will be legal after ten years if no action was taken by the land owner to reclaim his land? Are we witnessing the most dangerous precedent case in our land laws since its inception in circa 1862?"

I would say that 'Inoke's question not only conveys his personal concern, but also represents a general concern in the minds of many Tongans in the diaspora.

Fonua pe Tangata in relation to Matthew 4

Matthew 4 indicates a transition of Jesus' ministry, as well as a change in the geographical location where this ministry is going to be exercised. The words of verses 12-14 show that transition:

> "When Jesus heard that John had been put in prison, he withdrew to Galilee. Leaving Nazareth, he went and lived in Capernaum, which was by the lake in the area of Zebulun and Naphtali— to fulfil what was said through the prophet Isaiah."

The last verse of this section of Matthew, verse 25, says:

> "Many people from Galilee, the Ten Towns, Jerusalem, Judea, and the land across the Jordan River followed him."

It seems to me that in this passage, the author has a special interest in the connection of the land, the people, and the kingdom/reign of God. It shows in his selection of the passage from the book of the prophet Isaiah, as part of his claim for the fulfilment of the Old Testament prophecy. He saw the coming of Jesus to the lands of Zebulun and Naphtali, which had been grabbed by the Roman

Empire, as a fulfilment of God's plan for liberation. The quote from Isaiah carries that thought:

> "Land of Zebulun and land of Naphtali along the sea, beyond the Jordan River. This is Galilee where the non-Jewish people live. These people who live in darkness will see a great light. They live in a place covered with the shadows of death, but a light will shine on them." (Matthew 4:15-16)

The author saw the coming of Jesus as an agent for the advent of God's kingdom, for the purpose of liberating both the people and the land from land grabbers, namely the Roman Empire. This act of liberation aims for a transformation of the heart and behaviour among the law and policymakers of the day – the Roman Empire. Jesus' message truly identifies his intention:

> "Repent, for the Kingdom of the Heaven has come near." (Matthew 4:17)

Although the tribes of Zebulun and Naphtali are part of the ten lost tribes of Israel as claimed by historians, the author insists that the connection of their history and stories to their land must never be forgotten. As well as recording the author's political agenda in his gospel, he also noted the longing of the land itself to reconnect with its rightful land owners, even though they are here no more. It also reminds us of the Israelites conquest of Canaan and the rights of former land owners, whose names are long forgotten, to their occupied lands. William Barclay alluded to this:

> "Galilee's geographical position had affected its history. Again and again it had been invaded and conquered, and the tides of the foreigners had often flowed over it and had sometimes engulfed it." (The Gospel of Matthew Volume 1, p. 73)

Francis W. Beare has a contrary opinion in regard to these lands, and argues that in the time of Matthew, these two tribes had no cultural significance. He states,

"By the time of Matthew, the tribal areas had long since ceased to be of any importance; they were of no more than antiquarian interest." (*The Gospel according to Matthew*, p. 115)

This is a common view among those who are longing for land to grab or to occupy, like the colonial empires of our history. However, the coming of Jesus, according to the author of Matthew's gospel, is the fulfilment of Isaiah's prophecy for the reign of God to intervene and liberate this community from alienation and negligence.

Ulrich Luz also comments along those lines, by saying,

"Galilee consists of the 'Galilee of the Jews' and 'Galilee of the Gentiles.

Therefore our text concerns the sending of Jesus to the Jews, the people sitting in darkness, and to the Gentiles who are sitting in the land and shadow of death." (Matthew 1-7, p. 195)

This interpretation offers a broader view of the purpose of Jesus' ministry, which is inclusive and universal. His message of liberation is aimed at the heart, the centre of decision making. If the reign of God is taking place in the heart of decision-makers, then God's justice will be reflected through their actions.

The advent of the kingdom of God in the ministry of Jesus has an important connection with the liberation of the lands of Zebulun and Naphtali. Those who have been under the shadow of darkness and death are going to witness the dawn of a new day. As Isaiah prophesied for a Messiah to liberate those who were in exile, so it is with Jesus' ministry to this community. The author saw the purpose of the coming of Jesus as not only to bring light to the people who had been in darkness, because of their oppression, but also to put the spotlight on the land that had been taken away from them. Although their ancestors had long gone, their names were still alive in their lands. Their physical presence is gone, but their voices refuse to be silent in the text. Their voices are heard in the attachment of their names to their lands.

Fonua pe Tangata reading of Matthew 4:15

Now I am going to use *Fonua pe Tangata* concept as my lens to read Matthew 4 verse 15 from a Tongan migrant's perspective.

Firstly, the author insists that the connection of the land with the landowners is important, "The land of Zebulun, and land of Naphtali." The land bears the names of those who are assigned to care for it and any attempt to separate them, is not only an attempt to endanger the lives of people, but the existence of the land, as suggested by Rev Dr Nāsili Vaka'uta in his article "Voices of the Whenua: Engaging 1 Kings 21 through a Maori Lens," (p. 237-238)

Secondly, "The land of Zebulun and land of Naphtali" makes a connection between the land and their ancestors, the histories behind the land and stories that are told. When land is taken or when people are displaced, they are not only disconnected from their ancestors but also their histories and stories. This has occurred in colonial occupation of land around the world.

Thirdly, "The land of Zebulun and land of Naphtali along the sea, beyond the Jordan River:" gives us the impression that the people of the land (*tangata whenua/tangata'i fonua*) are always on the verge of travelling and exploring for new opportunities. Yet, they always maintain the connection with their lands through remittances, family reunions and important festivals that require them to return home, and by sharing their resources with those at home.

Fourthly, "The land of Zebulun and the land of Naphtali" demonstrates the significance of land as a home. To take away someone's land is an attempt to promote homelessness and landlessness. This is evident in places that have been colonized through exploitation, violence and manipulation. It is most upsetting when it is done by your own people, like the attempt by our own government in Tonga I have mentioned above, about the case in the *Matangitonga* newspaper on 22 March 2018.

The *Fonua pe tangata* concept gives a Tongan migrant like me the right to maintain my connection with our ancestral land in Tonga, and be passionate about the affairs that affect the people back home. It is also a reminder to the authorities in Tonga to take their hands off, and not to act as the colonial powers have done and are still doing around the world. It is not OK to separate the names of owners from their lands. I am glad the Land Law in Tonga still maintains the rights of the land owners, as it states on the Property Tonga website,

> "Some important points to understand about the Land Act of Tonga are that all land is the property of the Crown. The landholder's interest in any hereditary estate, tax allotment or town allotment exists as long as that person is alive and consideration often has to be made for any heirs."[12]

---

12. https://propertytonga.com/land-law-in-tonga.html

'Utu-longoa'a: A Voice from the Edge

The word 'utu refers to the rocks on the beach or shore. The word longoa'a means in English, "noisy or interrupting." When we combine these two words they become, utu-longoa'a, which means, "rocks that are noisy or interrupting." This term 'utu-longoa'a is derived from real life experience when the wind and waves strike rocks on the shore and produce a big commotion and loud noise. This noisy voice interrupts the silence of a peaceful evening. Although, this voice comes from the edge, everyone in the community, even those who live inland can hear and notice it. Everyone notices its sound because it is so persistent and vigorous. It is a loud voice that interrupts silence and the comfort of people.

This is the experience that our family had in the last seven and a half years when we lived in St Clair, close to St Clair beach in Dunedin. The noise caused by the winds and waves hitting the rocks sometimes interrupted our sleep. This is the nature of the rocks that are noisy, utu-longoa'a. However, sometimes the "voice from the edge" comes unnoticed, because it is an unfamiliar voice. It is sometimes confusing when it comes together with other voices.

The voice is a channel or an instrument that draws attention to someone's need. It is a familiar experience for babies to raise their voice when they are hungry, sick or feel sleepy. If someone dies in a family, the living members demonstrate their sorrow by weeping. Whenever any controversial issue occurs, people express their opinions by debating. They either use their voices to prove a point or to humiliate someone. When we are in a competition, the audience will either express their joy or disappointment by their voices.

Those who watched the Rugby League World Cup in 2018, might still remember the "sea of red" colour all over stadiums and rugby fields wherever the Tongan team played their games. Tongan fans annoyed a lot of people through their support of their team, Mate Ma'a Tonga. The most annoying of all was their loud voices. They were very noisy in their singing, chanting and cheering. Although, they are a minority community, their voices were heard not only in New Zealand, but around the continents of the world. Their voices were heard because they were determined and persistent in support of their team.

'Utu-longoa'a denotes the voice from the edge or the margin. It is a persistent voice that it is determined to be heard and recognised. It doesn't satisfy or accept the way it is treated by those who are at the centre. Usually, the voice from the edge is ignored and side-lined, but it refuses to surrender or retreat. It strives to interrupt the silence and to overcome all obstacles in order to be acknowledged.

The edge is where the weak, the powerless, and the poor are settled and find their home. They settle in that space either by their own choice or by force. Although, they are at the edge, they choose never to remain silent, but rather they are determined to make their voices known and heard. In making their voices known, they break the silence of the dominant and powerful voices. Furthermore, they also refuse to surrender to those dominant voices.

Walter Brueggemann, an Old Testament scholar, in his book entitled, *Interrupting Silence*, writes,

> "We now live in a barbaric world where the stones cry out against the violence that spirals from the top down. Our work is to join their refusal of silence and their brave insistence on voice."

Brueggemann statement is right and continues to be right if those who have voices to speak continue to be silent. We have a lot of examples in the world of those who are on the edge of the society, but have the right to speak out for justice for all.

When the new Government presented their Budget to our nation, I looked at it seriously and asked some critical questions:

- Does this budget address the needs of the powerless voices in our nation?

- Does it consider the welfare of those on the edge of our society?

When leaders of the powerful nations in the world had their meetings about their trade and businesses, I asked these questions:

- Are they aware of the pollution caused by their industries?
- Do they understand global warming and its impact on the rising of the sea level in the Pacific?
- Do they listen to the voices of smaller nations in the Pacific who are already submerged under the sea?

I doubt whether these voices will be heard from the centre, or from the top, to use Brueggemann's concept of power from the top. But these voices won't surrender or retreat until justice is served – and that is the nature of 'utu-longoa'a.

The story of the Canaanite woman and her meeting with Jesus is a classic example of a voice which resists being silenced until her hope and aspirations are acknowledged (Matthew 15:21-28). The woman was a foreigner (a Canaanite), a widow, a mother of a sick girl and she met Jesus at the border. She had heard about Jesus and his power to heal. She pleaded with Jesus to heal her daughter, but the text tells us that Jesus was silent. His disciples urged Jesus to chase her away. When Jesus spoke, he said to the woman,

"I was sent only to the lost sheep of the house of Israel."

When he spoke for the second time, Jesus said to the woman,

"It is not fair to take the children's food and throw it to the dogs."

Although, the woman was offended, she was not silenced. Neither did she retreat. She persisted until her voice was heard. In the end, Jesus heard the voice of a woman on the edge, and said to her,

"Woman, great is your faith! Let it be done for you as you wish."

And her daughter was healed instantly.

In the month of May the Tongan churches in Tonga and abroad, celebrated *Faka-Me* to commemorate the uniqueness of young people and children in the life of the church.

This is an indication that they are not just members, but very significant members. They are the most vulnerable members of our society. According to the Child Poverty Monitor research done in 2017 there are still 290,000 New Zealand children – around 27% of all children – living in income poverty.[13] *Faka-Me* is an opportunity to make their voice heard again and to interrupt the silence among the decision and policy makers of our nation. I just want to share a voice from the edge, a voice that will never be silent until it is heard – for that is the nature of *'utu-longaʻa*.

This is my last article for the *Connections* column and I would like to acknowledge the role of Rev Ken Russell in organising the roster of the contributors. I would also like to salute all my colleagues who have contributed to this column for your expertise and thought provoking words which have inspired and challenged me over the years. I have to admit that most of the articles that I have written in this column have come out of my personal experience of the area that my family and I lived by during the last seven and half years, St Clair beach. I just wanted to share a voice from the edge of our great City of Dunedin, a voice that will never silent until is heard – for that is the nature of *'utu-longoaʻa*.

---

13. https://www.occ.org.nz/publications/news/child-poverty-monitor-2017-media-release/

Conclusion

Please accept my humble thanks for coming onboard with me on my double-hulled canoe to hear my story (*talanoa*) while we are all on this voyage. I would like to say that my story is not the only story to tell. There are many stories which those who haven't heard them would love to hear, especially during this post-COVID-19 time. Because the nature of telling stories in the Tongan context is informal, it allows interruption, in Tongan, *kauitalanoa*.[14] This is a moment during the storytelling where one of the listeners can ask a question, make an affirmation, or make a point in an argument. The listeners then shift their attention and focus from the storyteller to the person who has interrupted. By allowing that shift to happen there is an opportunity for more voices and stories to be heard. Furthermore, those voices will express different opinions, which help to critique the story being told, and create a more balanced view of the story. Some of us experience this kind of interruption during church meetings or in a classroom. This can be annoying, but at the same time, can take the conversation to another level that creates better understanding.

One of the issues that migrants experience in a foreign land is the question that the Israelites asked during their exile in Babylon, "How can we sing the Lord's song in a foreign land?"[15] This question is real for those who have left their countries of birth and brought their faith with them into their adopted countries. The nurture of their faith and practice of their ministries have to be shaped in new ways in the new context. The challenge is that to create understanding in the new context, they have to find new ways to adapt and connect. *Fisi'inaua 'i vaha* can be a channel or a window that enables dialogue between the migrants and their new contexts. It is a concept that promotes the liberty of migrants to maintain their cultural identity while they are exploring new ways of being church in their new environment. It's a constant dialogue that the migrant communities have to endure in their new contexts.

---

14 *Kauitalanoa* refers to someone who interrupts in the middle of a story telling. This person is either asking a question for clarification or for a purpose of argument (in Tongan *tālanga*). Sometimes the result can be fulfilled and other times can be disruptive.

15 Words from Psalm 137 verse 4.

The Methodist Church of New Zealand, *Te Haahi Weteriana O Aotearoa* has a special identity, which it calls the bi-cultural journey. This is a journey of two cultures in one church, namely, the *tangata whenua*, under the leadership of *Te Taha Maori* and the rest of the ethnic groups, under the leadership of the *Tauiwi Committee*.[16] Some members of Te Haahi find this concept new and unfamiliar, especially those who have recently arrived from other countries, and joined the Methodist Church of New Zealand. However, this bi-cultural journey is framed to create unity in a church that is culturally diverse. It encourages people from cultures other than Europeans, to enjoy worship in their mother tongues and in styles that suit their inclinations. In addition, they are allowed to express their theologies in ways that reflect their cultural values and their faith in Jesus Christ, and at the same time connect with their local contexts. If our theologies are not connected with our local contexts, our practice of ministry is likely to be less effective.

Fisi'inaua 'i vaha would love to encourage both lay and ordained people to value their local contexts as a point of reference in their interpretation of Biblical texts and practice of ministry. We must know our local environment, and be aware of the social issues that affect individuals, families and our global household. We can then create a theology and meaning that are pertinent to our contexts, and also potentially provide solutions that address the social issues we face. Jesus was a good storyteller. He told his stories in the form of parables which we can read in the synoptic gospels.[17] His stories were constructed from his local environment, to address local issues that affected his local audience. Surely, Jesus' method of teaching reminds us of the importance of constant interaction with our audience and the issues that they face in their local contexts. Therefore, as migrants we are not isolated but very much part of our local community and its surroundings. We are an integral part of this voyage in the *vahanoa*.

---

16 *Te Taha Maori* is the section in the Methodist Church of New Zealand that overseas the ministry of the Maori people. The *Tauiwi Committee* is the other partner in the Methodist Church of New Zealand that overseas the ministries of other ethnic groups (Samoans, Fijians, Tongans, Europeans, Koreans, Rotumans, etc).

17 Matthew 13; Mark 4; Luke 8:4-15; 10:25-37; 15.

Bibliography

Books and Periodicals

Beare, Francis W., *The Gospel According to Matthew*, USA: Harper Collins Publishers; 1982.

Barclay, William, *The Gospel of Matthew (Vol. 1)*, Philadelphia: The Westminster Press; 1975.

Brueggemann, W. *Interrupting Silence*, Kentucky: Westminster John Knox; 2018.

Carter, Warren, *Matthew and the Margins*, London: T&T Clark International; 2000.

Churchward, C. Maxwell, *Dictionary Tongan-English, English-Tongan*, Nuku'alofa: The Government of Tonga; 1959.

Davidson, Jim, *Effective Time Management*, Michigan: Human Sciences; 1978.

Darragh, Neil, *Doing Theology Ourselves*, Auckland: Accent Publications; 1995.

France, R. T, *Matthew*, England: Inter-Varsity; 1985.

Fry, Ruth, *Out of the Silence*, Christchurch: The Caxton; 1987.

Frame, Janet, *Owls Do Cry*, Berkeley: Publishers Group West; 1960.

Gonzalez, Justo, *Luke*, Louisville: Westminster; 2010.

Gutenson, Charles E., *Christians and the Common Good*, Michigan: Brazos Press; 2011.

Havea, Sione 'Amanaki, "Coconut Theology" (p. 14-15), in *South Pacific Theology*, Australia: World Vision International South Pacific; 1987.

Havea, Jione, "Reading Islandly", *Voices from the Margin*, edited by R. S. Sugirtharajah, New York: Orbis Books; 2016.

Hau'ofa, 'Epeli, "Sea of Island", *The Contemporary Pacific, vol. 6, Number 1*, Suva: University of South Pacific; 1994.

Hu'akau, 'Inoke, "Illegal-activity vs time," *Matangitonga Magazine*, (March 22, 2018).

Hughes, Kent & Barbara, *Common Sense Parenting*, Illinois: Tyndale House Publishers, 1995.

Lewis, David, *We, the Navigators*, Honolulu: University of Hawaii Press; 1994.

Logan, Bruce, *Waking up to Marriage*, Christchurch: Maxim Institute; 2004.

Luz, U, *Matthew 1-7*, Minneapolis: Augsburg; 1989.

McConnell, William, *The Gift of Time*, England: InterVasity; 1983.

Moala, M, *'Efinanga*, Nuku'alofa: LALI Publications; 1994.

Morton, Helen, *Becoming Tongan*, Honolulu: University of Hawaii Press; 1996.

Nouwen, Henri, *Creative Ministry*, USA: Doubleday; 1971.

O'Donohue, John, *To Bless the Space Between Us*, New York (USA): Doubleday; 2008.

Rasbrooke, Max (edit), *Inequality – A New Zealand Crisis*, New Zealand: Bridget Williams Books; 2013.

Stott, John R.W, *Our Guilty Silence*, Bangalore: SAIACS Press; 1967.

Te Whariki by Ministry of Education, New Zealand: Ministry of Education; 1996.

Thomas-Tupou, S, "Telling Tales," *Faith in a Hyphen*, edited by Jione Havea and Clive Pearson, Australia: OpenBooks Publishers; 2005.

Tippett, Alan R. *The Deep Sea Canoe*, California: William Carey Library; 1977.

Tu'itahi, S, Langa *Fonua: In Search of Success*, Auckland: Pasifika@ Massey; 2005.

Tuwere, I. S, "Na Vanua, Lotu, Kei Na Mataniu Then, Now, and Where?", *Talanoa rhythms: Voices from Oceania*, edited by Nasili Vaka'uta, Auckland: Pasifika; Pasifika@Massey; 2010.

Vaka'uta, Nasili, "Voices of the Whenua: Engaging 1 Kings 21 through a Maori Lens," (p. 237-238), *Voices from the Margin*, edited by R. S. Sugirtharajah, New York: Orbis Books; 2016.

Watson, David, *Accountable Discipleship*, USA: Discipleship Nashville Resources; 1984.

Wilkinson, Richard and Pickett, Kate, *The Spirit Level*, London: Penguin; 2010.

Wishart, Ian, *Breaking Silence*, Auckland: Howling At the Moon Publishing Ltd; 2011.

Online and other sources

Christian World Service: https://cws.org.nz/

Child Poverty Action Group: https://www.cpag.org.nz/

Dunedin Abrahamic Interfaith Group and Otago Tertiary Chaplaincy 20 Annual Peace Lecture by Imam Afroz Ali, "Between Law and Spirituality: Islam's legal basis for its spirit of peaceful coexistence." http://www.dunedininterfaith.net.nz/peaceLecture16.php

Edmund Hillary and Tenzing Norgay: https://nzhistory.govt.nz/edmund-hillary-and-tensing-norgay-reach-summit-of-everest

FLO: Pasifika For Life and Le Va: https://www.leva.co.nz/our-work/suicide-prevention

Madeline Albright quote: https://quoterati.com/authors/madeleine-albright

Mornington Methodist Church Open Education Program by Professor Emeritus Colin Gibson on "Karl Jenkins, A Composer and a Conductor." http://www.dunedinmethodist.org.nz/

New Zealand Family Violence Clearinghouse: https://nzfvc.org.nz/

Right to Life New Zealand: https://righttolife.org.nz/

Save Children New Zealand newsletter and website: https://www.savethechildren.org.nz/

Glossary of Tongan Social and Cultural Concepts

Tongan term	English meaning/s
'Ata	Name one of the islands on the south-western side of Tongatapu
'Aupito	Very much
'Efinanga	A kind of Tongan basket
'uanga	Worm
'utu	Rock-face of coast, to get or draw water
Fakamā	Shame
Fala	Mat
Fānau	Children
Feau	Comfort
Femolimoli'i	To share our smallness
Fetoliaki	To pick here and there, to share a burden
Fisi'inaua	Waves' spray
Fofola	Unroll
Fonua	Land, womb, burial ground, people
Fue	Creeper plant
Hakau	Reefs
Holomui	Reverse
Inu	To drink
Kafo	Wound
Kāinga	Kinship, relatives
Kau	I / me
Kauitalanoa	Interrupting a story
Kimu'a	To the front
Ko au	I am
Ko hai	What
Laumālie	Spirit
Leveleva	Concluding, ending
Longoa'a	Noisy
Loto	Heart / soul

Māʻoniʻoni	Holy
Malanga	Herald, preaching, proclamation
Mālō	Thank you
Mālōlo	Rest, die
Masiva	Poor, poverty
Mate	Die
Mate maʻa Tonga	To die for Tonga
Mohe	Sleep
Momo	Crumbs
Ngāue	Working
Niu mui	Young coconut
Ongo	To be heard, to be felt
Pauʻu	Naughty, mischievous
Peau	Waves
Potopoto	Clever, skilful
Tahi	Sea
Taimi	Time
Talanoa	Storytelling, informal conversation
Tangaloa ʻAtulongolongo	God of the land
Tangaloa Tufunga	God of the sky
Tangata	Human, men
Tangilaulau	Lament, wailing
Taonakita	Kill your own self / suicide
Tatali pē	Waiting / being patient
Tatau atu	Respectful way of finishing or exiting after speaking
Tauhi	To keep, maintain, care
Taukakapa	Stretching to touch
Tongatapu	Main island of the Kingdom of Tonga
Ua	Two
Vā	Space in between
Vahanoa	Unknown / uncertain space
Vahevahe	Sharing, distribution
Vale	Crazy, silly

About the Author

Rev Siosifa Pole was born in the Kingdom of Tonga and brought up in the villages of Lapaha and Fua'amotu.

His parents were Kalafitoni and Neomai Kakala Nai Pole.

He was educated in Tonga and worked for the Tongan government before coming to New Zealand in 1986, for theological study at the Bible College of New Zealand, where he graduated with a Diploma in Ministry in 1989. Siosifa also holds a Diploma in Ministry from the Australian College of Theology, and a Bachelor of Theology and a Master of Theology from Melbourne College of Divinity. He trained for presbyterial ministry at Trinity Methodist Theological College in Auckland, with a focus on pastoral care and leading worship in English language settings.

In 2002 Siosifa was stationed to Wesley Roskill Methodist Parish, in Auckland. He was ordained in 2003 and served the parish for nine years. His second appointment was to Dunedin Methodist Parish where he served for seven and half years.

During his time in Dunedin, he started to write theological reflections from Tongan perspective to widen the understanding of this mainly *palagi* parish. Siosifa now serves as the Acting Director for Pasifika Ministries in the Mission Resourcing section of the Methodist Church of New Zealand.

The content of this book reflects Rev Pole's journey of ministry in the Methodist of Church of New Zealand, and also his desire to share his experiences as a Tongan migrant who is practicing ministry in Aotearoa New Zealand.

He is married to Naomi and they have four children.

Index

www.ingramcontent.com/pod-product-compliance
Lightning Source LLC
Chambersburg PA
CBHW071235020426

42333CB00015B/1487

9 781988 572512